THE ROAD TO
KONDOA

An Unexpected Journey With God

Appreciation for
The Road to Kondoa

The narrative of God reconciling humankind to himself comes alive when reading, "The Road to Kondoa." A God-breathed movement within this desolate place is history in the making. These men and women who listen to their God and trust in his timing are living letters permeating a difficult culture with Christ's love. Be inspired.

~ **Trudy Engebretson**
Pinehurst, North Carolina

"The Road to Kondoa" inspired, educated and moved me, and made me feel that I was a better person for having read it. Francine Thomas uses words much like an artist paints on a canvas. With every stroke of her pen she breathes life as she reveals God's nature and character in working out his master plan for the Gaula family and the people of Kondoa. I found myself stopping many times to reflect and praise God for who he is and for his amazing grace and power. "The Road to Kondoa" is a beautiful story of God's sovereignty, and a thrilling testament to what God can and will do through a life that is obedient to his will.

~ **Penny Terry**
Pinehurst, North Carolina

The Thomases, the Gaulas, and their precious mothers have joined King David in praise as they tell the story of how God has protected and provided for them in miraculous ways.

I will extol you, my God and King, and bless your name forever and ever. Every day I will bless you and praise your name forever and ever. Great is the Lord, and greatly to be praised, and his greatness is unsearchable. One generation shall commend your works to another, and shall declare your mighty acts. On the glorious splendor of your majesty, and on your wondrous works, I will meditate. They shall speak of the might of your awesome deeds, and I will declare your greatness. They shall pour forth the fame of your abundant goodness and shall sing aloud of your righteousness.

Psalm 145:1-7, ESV

~ Florence Werner
Gastonia, North Carolina

African symbol of the Ram's Horn stands for "humility" and "strength"

FOREWORD

There are no ordinary people. You have never talked to a mere mortal. Nations, cultures, arts, civilizations - these are mortal, and their life is to ours as the life of a gnat. But it is immortals whom we joke with, work with, marry, snub and exploit - immortal horrors or everlasting splendors.

~ C.S. Lewis[1]

C. S. Lewis wrote that one never meets an ordinary mortal. Surely this is true in Africa where seeds of greatness are all too often masked by the consequences of hardship and a life without love. Drunken fathers, self-seeking step-mothers/co-wives, forced marriages, antipathy between men and women, destructive cultural practices, tribal conflict and rampant disease fight to bury the African's potential.

In "The Road to Kondoa," Francine Thomas offers us the intriguing biographies of four ordinary people who manage to overcome seemingly impossible challenges to become God's extra ordinary sons and daughters. While their stories read like the dark fables of long ago, they are nevertheless very real. In each case, God's heroes and heroines wage a valiant fight to bring Christ to a dusty and poverty-stricken part of the world long dominated by malevolent spirits. The author masterfully weaves their individual yet interrelated stories in such a way that it would be impossible to miss the guiding hand of an all-knowing, all-loving, providential God. As a result, Given, Lilian, Vailet, Melina, and even the Thomases themselves, prove to be Lewis's "everlasting splendors."

As president of Empower International Ministries, I am proud to partner with the Thomases to bring light to a very dark world. Francine Thomas' reports from the field always bring me to tears. I believe you will have the same experience as you read these amazing stories.

~ Carrie A. Miles, PhD
President
Empower International Ministries

---

1. C. S. Lewis, *The Weight of Glory* (New York: HarperCollins Publishers, 1949), 47.

ACKNOWLEDGEMENTS

This book is dedicated to my husband, Dan, for his unquestioning love and unwavering belief in me. He never fails to remind me that with God, all things are possible. I also want to thank our children and grandchildren for allowing my story to influence their own walk before the Lord. They make me a better person. To them I pass down the legacy of my mother, Margaret King Miller, whose exemplary life of selfless commitment to God and family first inspired me to reach across the ocean to my brothers and sisters in Africa.

A simple "thank you" is not enough for those special friends who read my manuscript and offered an honest critique, and for my faithful intercessors who tirelessly prayed this project through to completion. I am also indebted to my granddaughter, Madeleine Joy Stoddard, who enthusiastically accepted the challenge of organizing and formatting the bibliographic material contained in this book. This is not her first foray into the world of publishing, nor will it be her last. God has gifted her in unique and special ways to share his great love through her own writing.

Finally, my deepest gratitude and heartfelt love goes to Given, Lilian, Melina, and Vailet for entrusting me with their precious stories that so beautifully reflect our Savior's tender care. My prayer for them and everyone whose efforts have contributed to the sharing of these accounts is that the Lord will bless them in rich and unexpected ways in their own divinely inspired journeys.

CONTENTS

A SPECIAL WORD
FROM THE GAULAS...

This is truly an inspirational account of our life story. I pray that it will serve as an invitation to a life of service to all who hear Christ say, "Come, follow me, and I will send you out to fish for people," (Matthew 4:19, NIV). I believe this work is an integral component of the Thomases' own missionary calling as well. As part of our story, they are letting the world know that "even the Son of Man did not come to be served, but to serve, and to give his life as a ransom for many," (Mark 10:45, NIV). I pray that we all choose such a path of obedience.

~ *The Rt. Rev. Dr. Given Gaula, Bishop of Kondoa*

I want to thank Francine Thomas for writing our stories. I never dreamed that even one person would find our lives interesting. Before I began reading the manuscript of this book, I bowed my head to pray. As I did, I saw a picture with the pages covered in blood. "What does this mean?" I asked God. "These words are covered by the blood of my Son, Jesus," he answered. Truly, God has lifted us up from nowhere in order to bring praise, glory and honor to him forever and ever. As the psalmist said so long ago, "May these words of my mouth and this meditation of my heart be pleasing in your sight, Lord, my Rock and my Redeemer."

Psalm 19:14, NIV

~ *Rev. Lilian Gaula*

Image from the Nations Online Project
Links to the World, http://www.nationsonline.org
Used by permission.

INTRODUCTION

While intriguing stories have emerged from many remote regions of Africa through the years, this book represents those of one special family whose accounts of God's supernatural intervention in their lives stir me like no other. Even though I have known the Gaula family for more than a decade, I have never been able to adequately explain why I feel so drawn to them. A few years ago, however, I received at least a partial answer when the Holy Spirit whispered that I was being given a new assignment. Out of my intimate friendship with the Gaulas would come the inspiration to "tell [the world] of all his wonderful acts" on their behalf (Psalm 105:2). This book is the result.

It is difficult to explain, but there is something decidedly different about being among those whose very existence is often tenuous at best. Despite having so little by western standards, the Tanzanians are a joyful people with much to teach outsiders about things that truly matter—family, friendship, community, love. I am no exception. God continues to use my African brothers and sisters to reflect new facets of his nature. Like the Pevensie children in C. S. Lewis' book series, "The Chronicles of Narnia," each time I return to Tanzania, I find myself standing on the threshold of my own comfortable existence about to enter a uniquely different world filled with mystery and challenge.[1]

This year is no different except that I have come with one paramount purpose in mind. I am here to interview four divinely chosen foot soldiers whose stories are mere footnotes in the annals of oral history certain to be lost over time. By God's grace, however, this is about to change as you meet the Gaula family. In truth they are ordinary people made extraordinary only by their unquestioning obedience to the challenge of God's call to spread the gospel message among a people largely unreached by western missionaries.

As a result of their efforts, many in Kondoa heard the name of Jesus for the first time in the early 1990's. Some have yet to hear his good news. The journey does not belong to the Gaulas alone, however. Their paths intersect many others along the way in a series of divine appointments, each one necessarily advancing the story of God's mercy and love for the people of this land.

This book is based on multiple conversations and numerous recorded interviews made over the course of several years. As a narrative biographer faced with the task of relating culture-specific life accounts, I have taken the liberty of translating conversations and dictations into language the western audience will understand. The principal's words in quotations represent my familiarity with them and the message they intend to convey. Due to my long and close friendship with the Gaulas, I will sometimes refer to them by their first names.

Admittedly, the challenge of adequately presenting God's sovereign acts in their lives is daunting. I know that absent the Holy Spirit my efforts will fail miserably. God's word assures me, however, that he will equip me "with everything good for doing his will," and that he will work in me "what is pleasing to him, through Jesus Christ, to whom be glory for ever and ever" (Hebrews 13:21). I pray these stories will inspire you, as they have me, to embrace greater and more daring adventures with God. As for that unseen hand, it is even now directing my steps to do all I can to preserve these glorious accounts for the generations to know that we do, in fact, serve a providential God who is very much alive and at work in and through his people today.

I invite you now to "taste and see that the Lord is good" (see Psalm 34:8) as you observe how the master planner moves people and events into position to achieve his eternal purposes. As my dear friend, Bishop Given Gaula, says repeatedly and often, "Come, come and see my people." I dare to add, "Come, come and see the sovereign hand of God."

Only be careful, and watch yourselves closely so that you do not forget the things your eyes have seen or let them fade from your heart as long as you live. Teach them to your children and to their children after them.

Deuteronomy 4:9

NOTES

1. Lewis, *The Chronicles of Narnia*, (HarperCollins Publishers, 1950).

PROLOGUE

A river is enlarged by its tributaries.

East Africa Proverb

Journal Entry, August 6, 2015

I lean forward in my seat eager to catch a glimpse of the dimly lit runway and terminal building below. At first, it is difficult to distinguish the airport lights from the small fires dotting the black landscape. Even as we descend, they appear only marginally brighter, and I silently applaud our skilled pilots who somehow manage to land without incident. They certainly earned their pay this night, I think to myself. After shouldering my backpack and following the other team members down the stairs, I pause on the tarmac to fill my lungs with the familiar scent of tropical flowers and smoky cooking fires. Ahh; I'm home.

Although I have passed through the Arusha/Kilimanjaro airport a number of times, I never cease to be surprised by its nondescript presence and lack of modern amenities available to western visitors setting out on their own grand adventures. I can't complain, though. I rather like the Casablanca-like mystique as well-used ceiling fans gently push warm air across worn wooden counters where travelers queue up to fill out forms for visas, immigration and customs. Somehow, it's all very comforting.

Our team eventually makes its way to the baggage claim area and out the main entrance to meet the Bishop's wife, Lilian, who has come to personally greet us. I can tell, however, that she has news she is reluctant to share. It seems the dilapidated 17 year-old Land Rover, long past its prime, barely made the long drive through the mountains and bush before breaking down. I can't say I'm surprised. Past experience has taught me that the faithful, but often ailing, vehicle requires lots of on-the-spot ingenuity to keep it going. This time, however, it is going to take more than baling wire, or a quickly fashioned cardboard gasket to get it up and running again.

We learn that the driver has left our transport at a repair shop in town in hopes the mechanic will be able to fabricate a necessary metal part in time to get us on our way. However, time here is relative. We will leave when the vehicle is ready. In the meantime, we decide to exchange our money for Tanzanian shillings before walking to a garden restaurant a short distance away.

Of course this delay is no surprise to God. In fact, he has gone before us to make every provision for our comfort and safety so that we might sit back and enjoy local cuisine surrounded by lush, fragrant flowers and the call of exotic birds. The hours tick by, and the evening air grows chilly. Still, we are reluctant to unload suitcases tied rather precariously atop our rented vehicle just to locate warm jackets. Instead, we move towards the only source of heat we can find—an outdoor pizza oven. We are delighted to discover that it offers just enough real estate to take turns standing around it while occasionally turning like so many chickens on a rotisserie.

Pleasant conversation, delicious food, and the beauty of the African night fill me with inexpressible peace. I look up to see God's handiwork magnificently displayed across the dome of the Southern Hemisphere and catch my breath. I almost believe that if I squint hard enough, I might just get a glimpse of God's hand masterfully painting the constellations on his heavenly canvas light years away. I can think of no better words to describe such splendor than those penned by the ancient psalmist. "The heavens declare the glory of God; the skies proclaim the work of his hands. Day after day they pour forth speech; night after night they reveal knowledge" (Psalm 19:1-2). I admit that I am almost sorry when the Land Rover finally turns its headlights in our direction some eight hours after our arrival. Although reluctant to leave this hidden paradise, I know God has even greater adventures in store for us as we begin our long, bumpy drive to Kondoa.

Before long, the tarmac ends forcing us onto deeply rutted dirt roads that are every bit as challenging as I remember. Frequently impassable roads are an integral part of the African experience. So, too, are the expected stops along the way as a territorial border guard heatedly cites some outlandish infraction of the law. We are only too aware that they often do this for the express purpose of lining their own pockets. If it weren't such an unnecessary hassle, it would almost be entertaining. I have never understood how these guards are able to keep a straight face when they accuse us of driving over the speed limit. Speed limit signs are rare, and without patrol cars or radar detectors, there is simply no way to gauge how fast anyone is traveling. Still, our driver has learned the hard way that it's useless to argue since it usually results in additional penalties. The best course of action is to beg for forgiveness while sweet-talking the official into accepting something more reasonable like a bottle of water and the equivalent of US $10, both of which the guard is sure to keep for himself.

Colorful slices of African life, even those that bring a bit of angst, remind to me to "give thanks in all circumstances, for this is God's will for you in Christ Jesus" (1 Thessalonians 5:18). I know that God is using every experience here in Africa, whether big or small, to mold me into a more worthy vessel fit to share his story with others.

part one

GIVEN

*It is doubtful whether God can bless a man
greatly until He has hurt him deeply.*

~ A.W.Tozer

1
Inhumanity

They are darkened in their understanding and separated from the life of God because of the ignorance that is in them due to the hardening of their hearts.

Ephesians 4:18

I sit silent and still in my chair, reluctant to make even the slightest of sounds. A small voice recorder whirs softly beside me ready to capture the words of the burly black man who will soon be taking his seat across from me. After several years of planning, I can hardly believe this moment has finally arrived. The first of four scheduled interviews is about to begin. As I wait, I take time to reflect on this strong man of God, and what he had to overcome to be where he is today.

By all rights, the Rt. Rev. Dr. Given Mzanje Gaula, Bishop of the Anglican Diocese of Kondoa, Tanzania, should be a mere statistic counted among so many others who have lost all hope for a better life. And yet he is not.

Through the many faithful prayers of his mother, grace stepped in to show him a better way to live. Today, he travels the world to share how Christ's redeeming love is making a difference in a land where black magic, animism and radical Islam partner with a host of other destructive cultural practices to keep the people enslaved in ignorance and poverty.

The Bishop's task is not an easy one, for there is a seemingly impenetrable wall around the hearts and minds of many. A lesser man might turn back, but God's Word continually strengthens his resolve. "Be strong and courageous, and do the work. Do not be afraid or discouraged, for the Lord God, my God, is with you" (1 Chronicles 28:20). Unless and until God directs him otherwise, the Bishop is determined to evangelize the region and disciple believers so that they, too, may be willing to go where God leads them, even into the darkest of the enemy's strongholds.

Although I have known this man for many years, I suspect there are depths of God's mercy towards him I have yet to discover. There is no doubt in my mind that it is only because his steely determination has been forged in the fires of adversity that he is able to bring the hope of Christ to so many today. "Consider it pure joy, my brothers and sisters, whenever you face trials of many kinds, because you know that the testing of your faith produces perseverance" (James 1:2-3). I sense that Bishop Gaula will need to fight with every ounce of strength he has in order to battle the evil forces of Satan bent on destroying these people and this land. I pray that my friend's willingness to speak openly now will bring healing to countless others who have yet to know Christ's loving presence.

Before long, Given enters the room to settle himself for what promises to be a protracted time of questioning and sharing. I pick up my pen and paper while quickly glancing at the recorder to make sure it is still running smoothly. "Tell me about your childhood," I urge, knowing that it will be difficult for him to relive painful memories of so much undeserved suffering at the hands of his father.

Given was born to a hard-working, God-fearing mother and an uncaring, emotionally distant father. Even now, he has few, if any, positive memories of his father, Mzee Viligio Mazengo Gaula. From the time he was a young child, Given never saw his dad as anything other than an abusive alcoholic—a weak, irresponsible man either unable, or unwilling to provide even the most basic of necessities for his family. It was not unusual for Melina, Given's mother, and her two young sons to go days without enough food to suppress their hunger. What little money Viligio made, when and if he chose to work at all, was spent on cheap, locally brewed beer.

In truth, Given had little chance of pleasing his father from the very beginning. Even his premature birth on July 27, 1967, at the Nala dispensary near his family's home in Lugala, a small village near Dodoma, seemed offensive and a great source of shame to both father and clan. Steeped in superstition and ignorance, the villagers believed that any child born before its time was sure to bring bad luck. Even worse, the product of such a birth could not possibly be considered human, and should not be allowed to live.

The people insisted that Melina leave her tiny baby boy in the forest to be devoured by wild animals. In a great act of defiance, she ran with her newborn son to a nearby clinic where she knew of a kind missionary nurse from Church Mission Society who might be willing to provide the kind of medical care for him that she could not.[1] If the child lived, Melina would take him home regardless of what anyone around her thought. If he did not survive, only the endless beatings her husband inflicted would be able to distract her from her deep grief.

By God's grace, the child survived despite having developed a severe case of pneumonia. After almost two months, much of it spent in an incubator, he was at last well enough for Melina to take home. She had not yet named her child, but remembered that this same nurse had told her years before that she must name her first son "Given," for surely he would be a gift from God. Thankful the Lord had graciously given her son back to her, she agreed, and named her son accordingly. Melina felt blessed even though she knew Given would be subjected to a life of abject poverty and physical abuse.

Mother and child continued to endure much emotional and physical abuse through the years. Frequent beatings raining down on Melina often spilled over to her son. No one outside the confines of their home ever dared to intervene. Fellow clan members may even have thought that Melina deserved whatever harsh treatment came her way. After all, she shamed herself, her husband and his clan by carrying only one child to term. An endless cycle of miscarriages did little to commend her repeated efforts to produce an acceptable number of children to serve as field laborers for the family and caregivers for younger siblings. Although embarrassed that her husband had taken several other wives in an attempt to produce more children, Melina secretly hoped it meant she would not have to bear additional children with such a man.

Her worst fears, however, were realized when she discovered she was pregnant yet again. Would she lose this one, too? Against all odds, a second son, Michael, was born healthy and on time. Surely this would make Viligio proud and inspire him to be a better provider. Sadly, it did not. Viligio never had a kind word, or loving touch for any of them.

The neglect and deprivation continued unabated for many years until Melina's uncle finally decided he could no longer stand by while his niece and nephews were treated so inhumanly. In a courageous act of compassion, he reported Viligio to the local magistrate. What happened next would be appalling to most fair-minded people. The magistrate demanded that Melina and her sons appear in court to testify in the presence of their abuser. One by one, they quietly presented details of unmitigated suffering. How frightening it must have been for them to publicly lay out the horrific actions of the very one who sat glaring at them only a few feet away with the threat of violence brewing in his dark eyes.

Unfortunately, but not surprisingly, the magistrate was only too eager to be bought off. After setting a fine for TZS 500, roughly the equivalent of 50 cents at the time, he let the defendant go free, but only after making him promise to return with a more substantial bribe payment.[2] Viligio was well aware that failure to comply would result in considerable jail time. With few options for meeting the terms set by the corrupt court official, the unrepentant father quickly sold what little the family owned, including their meager supply of maize and millet.[3] It mattered little to him that this food was all that stood between his family and certain starvation. His immediate needs were clearly more important. When he still came up short, he "borrowed" cows from neighbors and sold them without the owners' permission. Then he ordered his sons to gather wood to make enough charcoal to sell in order to satisfy the remainder of the bribe payment.

As Given shares this story, I find I am at a loss for words. How could any parent be so self-centered, so morally bankrupt as to harm the very ones he is supposed to protect? Thinking this is one of the most dreadful stories I have ever heard, I soon discover how very wrong I am. The worst is yet to come as the Bishop peels back the layers of an even darker memory.

"One night shortly after our court appearance," he says, "my father ordered me to sleep in our house rather than in the outbuilding I usually shared with the other young boys from the village." Given had no idea that his father had already set a diabolical plan in motion until he heard the ominous words, "I have been warning you, but you don't hear me. Today you will die." Wanting desperately to believe his father was just trying to scare him, the youth soon discovered that the man did, indeed, have sinister plans in mind. A night of inconceivable horror was about to begin.

NOTES

1. The Church Mission Society, one of the most influential missionary societies of the Anglican Communion, first sent missionaries to Uganda, Kenya and Tanganyika in the nineteenth century. The Society understood the importance of providing education along with religious training in order to produce effective indigenous leaders as well as an educated laity.

2. TZS is the currency abbreviation for the Tanzanian shilling. The Tanzanian shilling is made up of 100 senti (Swahili for cents), and is often presented in the form x/y. In this form, the x represents the amount in shillings and y represents the amount in senti.

3. Corruption takes many forms among politicians and government officials even today. According to Bishop Gaula's published research, political leaders have *carte blanche* to accumulate wealth by any means without repercussion. The moral code of conduct for leaders as established by the Arusha Declaration of 1967 gave way to the new and damaging economic reforms of 1991. Political leaders who engage in corruption are known as mafisadi papa, or "notoriously corrupt sharks." Gaula, Given M., *The Gospel of Luke as a Model for Mission in an African Context: With Special Reference to Challenges of Mission in the Anglican Church of Tanzania.* Thesis. University of Auckland, NZ, 2012. Auckland: U of Auckland, 2012. Print. 2012.

2
Supernatural Intervention

You intended to harm me, but God intended it for good to
accomplish what is now being done,
the saving of many lives.

Genesis 50:20

"Come here," his father commanded in an angry voice, "and don't move." Even though at 15 years of age, Given was already a strapping young man standing head and shoulders above his father, he dared not disobey. He was well acquainted with his father's fierce temper, especially when he was drinking. Sadly, this was most of the time. Told to sit on the dirt floor, he forced himself not to struggle as his father wrapped a rope first around his ankles and then his wrists. Then he was forced to double over as his father bound his wrists and ankles tightly together. The nightmare was about to begin.

"You wanted me to go to jail," his father spit out menacingly. "Now you have to pay!" Throwing the end of the rope over a rafter positioned directly over the cooking fire, the angry man strained to hoist his son up until he was dangling just feet from the wood stacked beneath him. Next, he stoked the still-smoldering fire with purpose.

Given's mother cowered behind a wooden post swallowing sobs that threatened to break loose as rivulets of tears coursed down her lined face. Her husband warned her not to utter a sound, or make any move to interfere. If she didn't obey, she would meet a similar fate. As if to leave no doubt that he would carry out his threat, Viligio placed a large machete on the floor next to the fire ready to pick up on a moment's notice if Melina should be foolish enough to attempt to free her son.

The poor woman was faced with an unthinkable choice. If she tried to save her son, they would both be murdered, and there would be no one left to care for her younger son. If she did nothing, she would forever live with the cruel memory of helplessly standing by as her son writhed in pain until the flames finally consumed his flesh. Her heart cried out to God for mercy in silent waves of inexpressible anguish.

I try desperately to keep myself from picturing the details of that awful night, but am unsuccessful. As the horrific scene plays across my mind, I can't help but think about another mother whose grieving heart was also shattered into a thousand pieces as her Son hung helplessly from a cruel wooden cross more than 2,000 years ago. It was a sight no mother should have to endure, and yet for the mother of Jesus, it was ordained.

Somehow I manage to pull my attention back to the present as the Bishop continues to describe the utter terror he felt as the rope that was holding him began to unravel. Just when he was certain his life was about to end, something happened that defies any reasonable explanation. Instead of dropping directly into the fire, he fell well away from the hot flames. It was as if an unseen hand had knocked him safely out of the danger zone. Just as Given was sure his father would move in with his machete to finish the job, the man inexplicably stepped to one side.

"You are lucky tonight," he muttered before walking away. "I wanted to kill you." It wasn't luck, but by God's grace that Given survived, even if badly affected by the toxic smoke. After a night spent struggling to breathe, at first light he stumbled to the nearest dispensary where he was immediately treated for severe smoke inhalation. "I will never forget that terrible time,"

Given says. "The wound will always be there. It was such a bad time in my life."

Although the memory of that night haunts both mother and son to this day, they are convinced that what happened was nothing short of miraculous. God had, indeed, watched over them just as he had when the three Hebrew men were ordered into the fiery furnace and Daniel was thrown into the lions' den. It was becoming increasingly clear to Melina that God had a special purpose in mind for her son beyond anything she could have imagined. The small seed of hope planted in her heart three years earlier when evangelists came to their small village, began to sprout and grow.

It was 1980. Two evangelists, both products of the East Africa Revival (EAR) movement, came to town to conduct an outdoor crusade. For seven days and nights, large crowds gathered from surrounding villages to hear the living Word of God preached without apology or reservation. Their message was one of loving tenderness. "Come to me, all you who are weary and burdened, and I will give you rest" (Matthew 11:28). They spoke of a deity far different than any they had ever known. Unlike the vengeful gods of their African Traditional Religious system, this God offered unconditional love and mercy.[1]

The fires of the East Africa Revival were ignited in 1929 when Dr. Joe Church, a white evangelical Anglican missionary doctor, joined a Ugandan friend to study Scripture and pray. They longed for a deeper infilling of the Holy Spirit, and a more intimate relationship with God. They were so transformed by their experience that Dr. Church eagerly returned to his mission station in Gahinia, Rwanda, to share what had happened. From this humble beginning, small groups of African preachers began to spread throughout Uganda, Kenya, and Tanzania preaching a message of repentance and the remission of sin through the shed blood of Jesus Christ. Their efforts resulted in unprecedented church growth from the 1940s until the 1970s. The legacy and influence of the EAR continues to impact churches today.

Although only 13 years old at the time, Given's heart was deeply moved by their powerful message. When the invitation came to move forward and kneel in repentance, he eagerly did so. That very night, he came to know Jesus as his personal Savior. He understood without being told that he had to forgive his father. And even if he never heard his father say he was sorry, it wouldn't matter. He would forgive him seventy times seven knowing that Christ died for all sinners, including his father. "For if you forgive other people when they sin against you, your heavenly Father will also forgive you. But if you do not forgive others their sins, your Father will not forgive your sins" (Matthew 6:14-16).

Given didn't realize it at the time, but God would use every painful experience in his life to forge a strong character with resolve enough to tell everyone he came in contact with that Jesus would never forsake them. "These [trials] have come so that the proven genuineness of your faith—of greater worth than gold, which perishes even though refined by fire—may result in praise, glory and honor when Jesus Christ is revealed" (1 Peter 1:7). The young boy did not know what his future held, but God did. He had much more to teach Given about his boundless mercy and grace.

The Gaula family never seemed to have enough to eat. There was a time later that year, however, that their situation seemed especially desperate. "I had eaten very little for days, and was terribly hungry," Given says. "My mother and I decided that since we had exhausted our current supply of customers in the area, I should go to a village some distance away to sell whatever amount of guava I could gather." If all went well, Given would earn enough to purchase flour for his mother to use for cooking. He could almost taste her delicious *ugali*, the thick porridge that is a staple in much of Africa. Perhaps there would even be enough for her to make the delicious pancake-like flatbread known as *injera*. If he was unsuccessful, the family would continue to go hungry.

Dumping the fruit into two metal buckets suspended from either end of a long pole balanced across his shoulders, a barefoot Given set out across the dense forest. His load soon became too heavy to carry. Even though he couldn't bear the thought of returning home empty handed, he was simply not strong enough to go on. With no better plan in mind, he did the only thing he could do. He settled under a tree, and let the night close in around him.

"Before long," he says, "I heard the call of the hyena and other dangerous animals I couldn't identify coming towards me in the dark." With nowhere to run or hide, he remained perfectly still. Somehow sensing the presence of promising prey, the creatures moved closer to sniff out the foolish intruder who dared to invade their territory. "They were so close they should have discovered me and torn me limb from limb," Given explains. "Instead, they turned around and left."

"What do you make of their strange behavior?" I ask him, even though I think I know what he'll say. Without hesitation, he tells me that God had dispatched angels to surround him with a cloak of invisibility. "If they had not protected me," he adds, "the lions and hyenas would surely have had a tasty meal that night."

The young boy was still trembling, when out of the darkness, a group of men emerged from the trees. They moved closer and closer to where he remained huddled on the ground. Each man was carrying a weapon—a spear or gun—to use in fighting off lions, or some other marauding predator known to roam the area. Although it was too dark for them to make out his form, the men sensed his presence just as the animals had earlier. "Is this a man, or a bad animal?" one called out. "I am a man," Given replied loudly. He knew that if he did not respond quickly, they would assume he was a deadly beast lying in wait with killing on its mind. Given had escaped the threat of animals. Now he was faced with another danger, but this time it was from humans.

"Why are you here?" they questioned when they saw he was but a lad. "Why have your parents allowed you to carry such a heavy load?" They seemed even more interested in understanding why he was traveling alone along this dangerous path that even adults avoided whenever possible. Before he had time to answer, one particularly observant man turned to his companions silencing their questions. "Can't you see that he's suffering?" he announced calling attention to the boy's thin frame. "He is starving, and has no clothes, or food." Given quickly explained that he had been sent to sell guava to make enough money to buy flour for his family. They were surprised by his courage and apparent desire to help his family. "This young man has compassion for his mother," one of them said. "I think in his life he will always help his mom." With that prophetic word, the men picked up his buckets, and they all set out together—several strong men and one not-so-strong young boy.

"We walked all night, perhaps 20 miles or more," Given recalls. "When the sun came up, the men asked if I could manage to go the rest of the way by myself. After assuring them he could, they turned to go in another direction. The truth is," Given admits, "I was reluctant to inconvenience them further. I knew that I could not manage by myself, although I did try. The load was just too heavy." Thankfully, other sojourners soon came along and helped him carry his produce to the nearby village. Wanting to thank them in some way, Given shared his precious guava with them. Gathering the few pieces of fruit that remained, he hurried to Kizota Primary School hoping to sell what was left to the students gathered on the playground.

Unfortunately, the thin, exhausted young boy was no match for the mean-spirited gang of children who found great pleasure in taunting him and stealing his fruit. Escaping with only a handful of guavas, Given was able to sell enough to passersby to purchase five kilos of flour, approximately eleven pounds. It was not nearly as much as he hoped for, but it was certainly more than they had.

Sleep-deprived and penniless, the young boy was steeling himself for the long walk home when he spotted a passing cart heading in the same direction. Trying to stay out of sight until the last possible moment, he hopped onto the back of the flatbed as quietly as he could, desperately hoping the driver wouldn't notice him. Without the means to pay the required five shillings for his ride, he remained low and as still as possible. Just before the vehicle reached Nala, Given quickly jumped off. He might have gotten away without notice except for one thing. He lost his footing and fell face down in the dirt, hurting himself badly in the process. His sharp cry of pain alerted the driver who began to shake his fist above his head demanding that the fleeing boy come back to pay for his ride. Knowing it was not right to run off without paying, the young Given had no choice. He ran away as fast as he could. Later on, when he had time to think about all that had transpired since he left home, he knew it was only by the grace of God that he had survived the day. At any given point, he could have lost his life, or been badly injured.

So do not fear, for I am with you; do not be dismayed, for I am your God. I will strengthen you and help you; I will uphold you with my righteous hand.

Isaiah 6:41:10

34

1. There are four foundational religious beliefs in the traditional religions: (1) the belief in impersonal (mystical) power(s); (2) the belief in spirit beings; (3) the belief in divinities/gods and (4) the belief in the Supreme Being. These foundational religious beliefs are essential to our theological interpretation and analysis of the traditional religions. Any meaningful and effective Christian approach to the traditional religions must begin from here. Turaki, Yusufu, *Africa Traditional Religious System as Basis of Understanding Christian Spiritual Warfare*, Lausanne Movement. August 22, 2000. www.lausanne.org/content/west-african-case-study (accessed June 17, 2016).

3
Divinely Possible

*Faith sees the invisible, believes the unbelievable,
and receives the impossible.*
Corrie Ten Boom (1982-1983)

Godly leaders recognized that young Given had a special call on his life. When he was 16 years old, his pastor, Rev. Wilson Malebeto, urged him to continue his education beyond Grade 7, the minimum required by law. This was a necessary first step in the pastor's long-range plan to eventually send Given to St. John's College, Kilimatinde, a satellite campus of Msalato Bible College at the time. The pastor knew, even if his young friend did not, that such an environment would serve God's purposes for him in the years ahead. However, there were a number of hurdles to clear before this vision could be realized.

First, young Given would have to pass the national examination required for acceptance to secondary school. If he managed to do that, he would still have to find a way to cover the cost of uniforms, school fees and supplies, approximately US $40 per year. It might as well be $1,000 to a poor family like the Gaulas. Absent a miracle, it would be impossible to come up with so much money. Even if everything else fell into place, Given would most likely be assigned to one of the few government schools located many miles away. Along with scores of other children, he would have no choice but to walk long hours to and from school in the dark, arriving home late at night to complete his assignments by the light of a dim lantern.

Fearing the worst, Given knew he would be subjected once again to the kind of humiliation he and his brother had endured in the past when walking to school without shoes and only their mother's kanga cloths to cover their bodies. This was a source of great shame and embarrassment to the boys then, and he had no doubt it would be again.

Given might have given up, but his keen intellect fueled an unquenchable thirst for knowledge. He was justly proud of his rich tribal heritage that had been passed down through generations of storytelling, yet he longed to know more of life beyond the confines of his world. Education was an important key to making this possible. Without it, he knew that nothing would change.

Determined to find a way to enlarge his horizons, Given took advantage of every spare minute to make charcoal to sell as an inexpensive source of heating and cooking. Always Given's champion, Melina's commitment was as strong as her son's. She joined Given in his efforts to escape poverty by educating himself. She knew intuitively that this would be the springboard for a better life for her son.

The work was backbreaking and dirty. Both mother and son labored long hours gathering branches and cutting small trees. After collecting all they could, they would dig a deep pit to use as a kind of in-ground smoker. Occasionally, they layered the wood in a mound above ground. By lighting the wood and covering it with dirt, they could safely leave it to smolder for 3 to 15 days until nothing was left but a dark gray substance ready to be broken into chunks and bagged for sale. Each evening, almost before the first spirals of smoke escaped the piles, Given set off into the darkness to find additional work digging ditches for people to bury their dead. It is difficult to say which job was most distasteful.

A large portion of the money Given and his mother earned was set aside to buy him a shirt and pair of trousers. They saved some of it to pay for transportation to and from Kilimatinde Bible School. At one point, Given ran out of customers, so he asked a friend to take a bag of charcoal with him the next time he visited the more heavily populated city of Dodoma. Perhaps there he would find customers more eager to purchase this ready source of fuel they had no time to make for themselves. When Given's father heard about the plan, he decided to go along. Somehow, he was able to talk Given's friend into giving him the charcoal to sell. Of course, he had no intention of doing anything to help Given. He merely wanted the money to buy beer for himself. Given discovered the truth only after his friend returned home empty handed. It seems that once again his father had shamelessly put his own needs above those of his family. It was a bitter disappointment for the hard-working lad who wanted so desperately to make his dream of school a reality.

Utterly discouraged, he sought the advice of Rev. Malebeto once more. Although moved with compassion, the man of God was helpless to offer any financial assistance. However, he thought he might find an answer to Given's dilemma at the local offices of World Vision. In the early days of the organization, it operated in partnership with area churches to assist the most at-risk children. Given was certain that, when the minister explained his plight, the men of World Vision agreed to contribute enough money to buy books and pens for his classes.[1]

Still, their sacrificial contribution wasn't enough. Knowing he had to find the necessary funds to cover the bulk of the student's school expenses, Rev. Malebeto turned to the spiritual leader of the Anglican Diocese of Central Tanganyika, Bishop Yohana Madinda. The Bishop listened to what the pastor had to say, and perhaps even without fully knowing why, agreed to pay tuition and additional school fees for the boy. This proved to be the beginning of a long, supportive relationship between Given and the Bishop until the older man's death in 1989.

It wasn't only the seasoned men and women of God who helped to shape Given's life, however. The young people also had a role to play. When he was 18 years old, and a new student at Kilimatinde Bible School in the Anglican Diocese of the Rift Valley, Given roomed with other students in the men's dormitory. "I'll never forget my first full day there, September 4, 1985," he recalls. "An older student, Samuel Masine, awakened early that morning to share something very strange with me. 'Last night, I dreamed you had become a bishop,' Samuel said, 'and that there was a huge celebration.'" Samuel told Given that he had many dreams in his life, and while most came true, this one seemed just too improbable to be taken seriously. "How can you become a bishop?" he asked, and they both laughed. Although neither of them guessed it at the time, God did have very big plans for Given's future. A number of years would pass before Given had reason to remember his classmate's most unlikely dream.

Opportunities once thought out of reach for a poor black boy from a small African village eventually opened up to take Given first to Msalato Theological School in Dodoma, then on St. Philip's Theological College some 90 kilometers away in Kongwa, and later to Church Army Africa Carlile College in Nairobi, Kenya. Few friends, or family understood why he was chosen when others were not. Given and his mother, however, had no doubt that God was the one orchestrating every step. For what purpose, they were uncertain. Perhaps that was a kindness, for had Given known what lay ahead, he might have been tempted to run from God's call on his life.

While studying Mission Theology, Pastoral Leadership and Development in Kenya from 1988 to 1989, Given was selected to serve as assistant to the Diocesan Director of Mission and Evangelism. His duties included translating for the director, a native of New Zealand who spoke no Swahili, and helping to establish programs and strategies for evangelism and church planting in Kondoa. Little did he know that this assignment would pave the way for his future role as Bishop of Kondoa.

During his time at school in Nairobi, Given became the subject of what turned out to be a providential faculty discussion. At issue was whether the young student should be recommended for the priesthood. The principal was adamant that he was far too young to be considered. Surely there were older students more deserving of such an honor. As God ordained it, however, the heart of one faculty member was deeply moved. With tears in his eyes, he pleaded with the principal to reconsider. "Yes, he is young," he said, "but I believe God is calling him." His heart-felt words turned the tide, and before long, Given was one step closer to a future known only to God.

NOTES

1. World Vision International is an Evangelical Christian humanitarian aid, development and advocacy organization. With programs and offices in more than 100 countries. Founded in 1950, it is dedicated to working with children, families and communities to provide long-term assistance to overcome poverty and injustice. World Vision International. http://www.worldvisioninternational.com/n.p., n.d. Web (accessed 15 Feb. 2016).

4

God's Change Agents

For I know the plans I have for you," declares the Lord,
"plans to prosper you and not to harm you, plans to give
you hope and a future."

Jeremiah 29:11

G iven seemed to have an innate gift for knowing how to communicate the love of Jesus with genuine passion and excitement. Never one to be shy, he eagerly shared his testimony with anyone who would listen. Everyone who heard his story was understandably amazed. Instead of expressing bitterness for the hardship he endured, he spoke only of love and compassion for others. "If God could make such a difference in my life," he would say, "he can certainly do the same for you."

Even though Given was young and inexperienced, the Bishop felt that he had a special talent for preaching. He decided to give him an opportunity to hone his skills in a region that had not yet been reached with the Gospel. Kwamtoro, an administrative ward of the Kondoa district of the Dodoma Region, was a Muslim community known to be extremely resistant to outsiders. When the young lay pastor arrived, the people made it clear they didn't want to hear his message. After a time, it was evident he would have to move on, so the Bishop made plans to send him to minister to the people of Tarkwa, located some 45 miles from Kwamtoro. Although the people there followed African Traditional Religions, they were at least open to his message. They had already heard about this Christian God from a teacher at the local school. If nothing else, it would only require them to add one more god to their roster of deities. No problem.

As it turned out, there was no place for Given to find lodging in the village. He was forced to look elsewhere. The only place he could find was an abandoned structure miles away in the southern region. The run-down shell of a mud house was in a terrible state of disrepair. Only a few walls remained standing, and the thatched roof had long since fallen in. With no alternative, Given slept on the dirt floor without protection from either the elements, or the wild animals. Undaunted, he woke each morning eager to share the gospel with any and all who would listen. Soon, there was a small, but vibrant congregation flourishing under his care.

At the time, missionaries from New Zealand were working and living in Kondoa. David and Jen Pearce were actually the first outsiders to bring the gospel to the area. When the Bishop told them of Given's ministry and his new converts in Tarkwa, David and one of his elders agreed to go there to conduct a service. They were prepared to baptize new believers for this young pastor who, because he was not yet ordained, could not officiate the rite. They were told that Given lived quite a distance away from the worship site, so on their way, they planned to stop by to give him a lift. When David saw the young man's living conditions, and learned that he had to walk 70 miles or more to reach the distant village, he wept with compassion. He made up his mind to write to the Bishop and ask that the selfless young pastor be allowed to live with him to assist in the work in Kondoa. The Bishop was only too happy to agree to such a proposal.

The seasoned missionaries happily worked alongside their young protégé for the next three years evangelizing the Muslim population. It was an extremely difficult and discouraging time. That is, until one memorable encounter changed everything.

The threesome made plans to plant a church in the eastern part of the district, and even found a Christian teacher and his wife who were willing to lead services until other arrangements could be made. With great anticipation, they set a date for the opening service with David and Given officiating. However, when they arrived, no one was there, not even the teacher. Thinking that the lay pastor must have forgotten, or perhaps had gone into town to get supplies only to be delayed, they waited for a time before driving away somewhat disheartened.

Nearing a small village, they saw a large group of people standing around a woman on the ground. They stopped to see what was going on, and discovered the woman to be the wife of the local imam, the Islamic worship leader of the local Sunni Muslim community. The relatives standing watch around her explained that she was chronically anemic, and that without proper medical attention, she might not survive. As a last resort, the family members had carried her out to the road much earlier hoping that a passing car would stop to take her to the nearest hospital. "They had just about given up hope when we came by," Given tells me.

It is important to note that in those days, few people had cars. Most traveled on foot or by bicycle. Why, then, I wonder, would the relatives even think about taking the woman out to the road with hopes of catching a ride? Apparently, the missionaries were the only ones with a car to pass by that spot in the road all day. "If the service at Tarkwa had taken place as planned, we wouldn't have been driving this road at this particular time." God was definitely orchestrating events. Anxious to hear the rest of the story, I urge him to continue.

"We quickly loaded the woman and several of her relatives into the back of our car, and sped off towards the nearest medical facility." After tests at the hospital revealed the gravity of the woman's situation, doctors determined that she needed an immediate transfusion of blood. Each person in her entourage was tested to see if there was a suitable match for her blood. There wasn't. "Not one black person, including me," Given explains, "had the same type blood as this woman." It seemed that all hope was lost when David suddenly stepped forward to insist that he be tested just as the others had been. Imagine everyone's astonishment when the results showed a perfect match! The nurses quickly took his blood to transfuse the dying woman. Given and David began to pray in earnest, and after some time, the woman miraculously rallied.

"Think about the significance of this event," Given says looking at me intently. "It was the first time these followers of Mohammad had ever known a man to give his blood for a woman. Not only that, but here was a white man who willingly gave his blood to a black woman. It wasn't just any white man, though. It was a white Christian man who donated his blood to save a black Muslim woman." David's actions had an astonishing impact on all those in the room.

Without warning, the sheik stood up, pointed to David and Given, and said, "You are a servant of Allah!" It mattered little to him that they were obviously not of the same faith. Their compassionate disregard for social conventions had won his respect as well as the respect of all who were present. The sheik knew that, above all else, they were good, caring people. They would make good neighbors. That seemed to settle the matter.

Still, David didn't want any misunderstanding, so he insisted that Given tell them they were not servants of Allah. "We are servants of Jesus!" Given boldly announced. The Muslims were nonplussed by such a declaration. As far as they were concerned, they were friends.

From that moment on, the Muslim community welcomed all new Christian church plants with open arms. Over the next several years, 17 churches were established in the area. As in the parable of the good Samaritan recounted in Luke 10:25-27, one act of selfless concern for a fellow human being opened a door to the gospel in a way that nothing else could. Simply put, these men of God showed their love for others because Christ first loved them. "This is the very best way to love. Put your life on the line for your friends" (John 15:13, MSG).

On one other occasion, Given and David discussed taking the gospel message to the Islamic village of Panguroa. Once the decision was made, they asked the village sheik for permission to show the Swahili translation of the "Jesus" film.[1] For reasons only God knows, the sheik agreed. However, when he saw that the duo had only a small, portable screen with them, he insisted they project the film against the whitewashed side of a warehouse building so that the entire village would have the opportunity to view it.

Villagers turned out in large numbers to investigate this very curious event. After all, no one had ever seen a film before, much less one about some man named Jesus. Soon men, women and, children gathered to take a seat on the ground in front of the sheik and his elders. All eyes were fixed on the scenes unfolding on the side of the building. That is until the Roman soldiers began to nail the horrible spikes into the hands and feet of Jesus. This was too much! The people began to weep and cry out. They did not understand that actors were merely playing the part of the real biblical characters. They truly thought that somehow, perhaps by some magic they did not understand, they were witnessing an actual crucifixion.

At this point, the sheik jumped up, and holding his long walking stick above his head, commanded everyone to be quiet. *Angalieni! Angalieni! Sikilizeni! Msikilizeni Yesu!* ("Watch, watch, listen, listen, listen to Jesus"), he said in a thundering voice.

How amazing it must have been to witness this devoted follower of Mohammed uncharacteristically urging his people to give their full attention to an account of the very man the Koran teaches was not crucified and, in fact, did not die, but was taken directly into heaven.[2] Such an unexpected response could only have taken place through the inspiration of the Holy Spirit. Although the sheik himself did not respond to the call to accept Jesus as Lord and Savior at the close of the film, he did allow a Christian church to be established. And so, the church at Panguroa was planted that very day. Today, it is a thriving, growing center for the teaching, preaching, and spreading of the remarkable message that Jesus died for the sins of all humankind, was raised to new life, and will come again to gather his own to live with him for all eternity.

God continued to use young Given in a mighty way to make his name known throughout the villages and countryside just as he had in Panguroa. Even though he felt a sense of fulfillment, however, there was something missing in the young man's life. He was lonely in spite of the satisfying work with the Pearces. The truth is that Given had a deep longing for a companion. In fact, he had been asking God for some time to provide a suitable wife for him, someone who would stand by his side in ministry.

It wasn't until he met Lilian Zakaria at Msalato Theological College in the school year 1986/1987 that he knew he had found the perfect woman to walk beside him into his God-ordained future.

In African society, the father is expected to negotiate the terms of the bride price. Given knew all too well that he would never be able to count on his father's help, so he began to set aside every bit of money he earned that wasn't needed to buy food for his family. He continued to dig ditches, make charcoal, and even sell the few vegetables his family could do without.

For eight years, Given saved whatever money he could, including the profit he made from selling his rickety old bicycle. In 1994, Given was resolved in his desire to propose to Lilian, the young woman he had met at school. He had saved TZS 45,000, approximately US $21 in today's economy. It wasn't much, but he thought it would be sufficient to meet any terms dictated by Lilian's father. Unfortunately, her parents did not know the character of Given's father when they sent word for him to meet with them to discuss a fair price. "I had no choice," Given explains. "I had to ask my father to meet with my future in-laws on my behalf." Viligio agreed, and after some haggling, the two families settled on TZS 56,000. Perhaps sensing that this was a lot to ask of such a poor family, Lilian's parents told Viligio that if he could pay 50,000 now, they would trust him to pay the rest later. With the 5,000 a friend loaned him, Given now had enough to make the woman he loved his wife.

Viligio agreed to return the following week to hand over the bride price to Lilian's parents. Given waited anxiously for news of his father's return, but after many hours passed and there was no sign of him, he became extremely concerned. After inquiring of his friends and acquaintances, he discovered that his father had been seen boarding a bus to Kongwa, presumably on his way to meet another woman.

"I was crazy with worry," Given says. Lilian also assumed the worst when Given's father didn't show up as arranged. "Why have you changed your mind about marrying me?" she tearfully demanded of Given. He quickly assured her that he had not changed his mind at all. In fact, quite the contrary was true. He assured her that he desperately wanted to marry her. Unfortunately, he had no idea where his father was, but secretly guessed he had absconded with the money, and was up to no good. Imagine the despair and anguish Given felt knowing that the money he worked so hard and long to save was most likely gone. Both Given and Lilian understood this meant the end of all their hopes and dreams.

It seemed all was lost until Given thought to appeal to his dear friends, David and Jen Pearce. Although he simply asked them to pray that God would somehow provide, they went the extra mile and gave him what little they had—TZS 30,000. Not knowing where he would get the rest, but trusting God to supply his need, Given returned to Dodoma.

On the way, he met his friend, Peter Candy. Peter had accepted Jesus as Lord and Savior after Given showed him the film first produced by the Jesus Film Project in 1979.[5] When Peter and his wife heard about the theft of the bride price money, they took pity on their friend, and gave him a heifer worth about TZS 20,000. Elated that the sale of this animal would bring him enough money to go through with the marriage, Given wondered who he might ask to act as his representative. He certainly wouldn't trust his father again, so he turned once more to Pastor Malebeto asking him to serve as his spiritual father in making the arrangements. The pastor agreed to represent him, and taking a trusted friend along as a witness, he set out to meet Lilian's parents.

As Given recounts this story, it occurs to me that he was still TZS 6,000 short. "I never had to pay that extra amount," he explains with a laugh when I ask about it. "Lilian's parents told me it would have gone to the village elders anyway as "smoking money." Apparently, this is the African way of making a joke. At any rate, the couple was greatly relieved that they could now post the banns of marriage, or the wedding announcement, at the local parish church. In spite of everything, God had worked everything together for the good of his two servants. He would continue to do so.

Over the years, Given has watched God faithfully provide exactly the help he needs at exactly the time he needs it the most. "Looking back now, I see God's hand more clearly," he says. "One day I was reading powerful words in the Bible that seemed to be written just for me. "Though I walk in the midst of trouble, you preserve my life. You stretch out your hand against the anger of my foes; with your right hand you save me. The Lord will vindicate me; your love, Lord, endures forever—do not abandon the works of your hands...your works are wonderful, I know that full well" (Psalm 138:7-8; 139:14b). He would count on these words many times in the years ahead.

NOTES

1. The "Jesus" film first premiered in 250 U.S. theaters in 1979. Its first international showing in Hindi was to 21 million Indian viewers in 1980. The first film teams were launched in the Philippines that same year. By 1984 the film was translated into 100 languages. The Jesus Film Project was officially founded in 1985. As of 2016, the Jesus Film Project has produced more than 30 short and feature length films. It has partnered with more than 1,500 ministries with more than 200 million viewers declaring Jesus as their Savior. The Guinness Book of World Records recognized the "JESUS" video as the "Most Translated Film" in history. Jesus Film Project, www.jesusfilm.org. (accessed June 17, 2016).

2. This story was recounted by David Pearce in his self-published book entitled, "Kondoa 31: One Man's Journey Through Life." The number "31" in the title refers to the telephone number of the Church of the Good Shepherd, the cathedral on the diocesan compound. Pearce, David, *Kondoa 31: One Man's Journey Through Life*. www.publishme.co.nz, 2015.

5

God's Man for the Hour

*And who knows whether you have not come to the
kingdom for such a time as this?*

Esther 4:14 (ESV)

In 2004, Given was awarded a full scholarship to The Virginia Theological Seminary and Divinity School (VTS) in Alexandria, Virginia, about 70 miles from where I lived with my husband, Dan, in the Shenandoah foothills. During his time in seminary, Given was assigned to assist in pastoral duties at St. Francis, a prominent Episcopal Church in affluent Potomac, Maryland. Each week he taught Sunday school classes and helped out wherever he was needed. No task was too great or too small. Although he had been a circuit priest overseeing 17 separate congregations in Tanzania, he had much to learn about how churches function in America. It was a fruitful, but sometimes perplexing education.

In the early fall of 2005, Rev. Robin Adams, pastor of The Church of the Word in Gainesville, Virginia, called the school to see if any students would like to join our congregation for the weekend at an Episcopal spiritual retreat center located in the Blue Ridge Mountains. Longing for a chance to get away from the busy campus and noisy traffic just outside the seminary's high brick walls, Given eagerly claimed this as a gift from God. How pleasant it would be to hike along the streams and beautiful tree-covered trails of the mountains. Besides, who knew what new friends he might make? God knew, as we were soon to discover.

My husband agreed to pick up the seminarian on his way home from Ft. Belvoir Army base where he worked so that he could ride with us to the retreat center. It seemed like such an insignificant gesture at the time. Little did we know that this "chance" encounter would prove to be the genesis of a long and divinely orchestrated partnership between our family and the Tanzanian people we have come to call our own. Over the next couple of years, Given, and later his wife, Lilian, who was attending a seminary in Pennsylvania at the time, visited our home as often as possible. They quickly became an integral part of our family.

After graduating from VTS in May 2006, Given returned to his homeland to assume a new position as Chair of the Mission Department at Msalato Theological College in Dodoma. Lilian remained in the States to complete her final year at Trinity School for Ministry in Ambridge, Pennsylvania. All these years later, I still wonder what their children thought about exchanging one parent for the other as first Given, then Lilian, answered God's call to higher education in a country so far away from friends and family. God did not forget the children, though. The influence and daily presence of their grandmother, Melina, during those early years provided the necessary stability to make sure they were cared for and well-grounded. Just as she had watched over her own son for so many years, she now was watching over his children.

A little more than a year after returning to Tanzania, Bishop Mhogolo selected Given for post-graduate study at The University of Auckland, New Zealand, starting in 2008. His intention was to eventually add Given to the faculty at St. John's University in Dodoma, an excellent school very much in need of boosting its accreditation. Understandably, study abroad was an opportunity Given didn't want to miss. However, he had been away from his wife and children long enough. He was determined not to leave them behind again. While his travel and living expenses were taken care of, he simply had to find a way to support his family so that they could accompany him. A plea went out to their many friends and family. People around the world, including my husband and I, responded by pledging financial support to cover their stay in New Zealand.

The next four years saw the family's faith tested in unusual ways. The challenges were many. First and foremost was the children's unfamiliarity with English. The language barrier made it especially difficult for them to make friends at the same time they were attempting to adapt to the unfamiliar, demanding British school system. It was certainly unlike anything they had encountered in Tanzania's schools. After awhile, though, they began to pick up the language as children do, and even make a few friends. By the end of their time in New Zealand, the children's Muslim classmates were bringing their own parents to the Gaula home on a regular basis to hear about, and later accept, Christ as Lord and Savior.

Although Given had picked up enough English in America to carry him through two years of seminary, his skills fell short of what was needed to successfully pursue a post graduate degree. How would he ever be able to author an academic book-length dissertation with all the unfamiliar nuances and rule exceptions of English? No one would have blamed him if he had just thrown up his hands in defeat. However, God had proved himself faithful many times over, and Given knew he would not let him down now. Putting his hand in God's, Given took one step at a time. He was not disappointed. Individuals with no other motive than that of responding to the Holy Spirit, stepped forward to oversee his efforts. One particular saint even offered to edit his dissertation. Now, that is a true act of love.

In 2012, after four years and much perseverance, Given earned the coveted Doctor of Philosophy degree. It is not by chance that he chose as the thesis for his dissertational work, "The Gospel of Luke as a Model for Mission in an African Context: With Special Reference to Challenges of Mission in the Anglican Church of Tanzania."[1] This important paper would later become the blueprint for his forward-thinking mandate for mission in Kondoa. By appropriating a specific hermeneutic, or method of interpretation, Given was able to demonstrate Christ's passion for the socially marginalized. This called for a careful reading of the Lukan text through the lens of the Tanzanian *ujamaa*, or communal ethos.

Julius Nyerere, a much-loved Tanzanian anti-colonial activist, politician, and political theorist, first popularized the term when he embraced ujamaa in an effort to institute a socialistic society that holds a person becomes a person through the people or community.[2] Given, on the other hand, used *ujamaa* to show that it is Christ, not others, who causes people to realize their full potential. In essence, Given set aside Nyerere's socialistic premise, but accepted his claim that people, particularly Christians, should work together to raise the standard of living in Tanzania. As he explained, the church needed to recover Luke's missiology, and expand its limited mission praxis to better reflect the mission of Jesus. In so doing, the church would be able to practice a holistic gospel mission capable of transforming the whole community.

Religion that God our Father accepts as pure and faultless is this: to look after orphans and widows in their distress and to keep oneself from being polluted by the world.

James 1:27

The Gaulas initially thought they would be returning to Tanzania to serve on the faculty of St. John's University located in their hometown of Dodoma. This was exciting for many reasons, not the least of which is that the proposed salary would raise the family's standard of living. God, however, had different plans. Even before they left New Zealand, a call came for Given to serve as Bishop of Kondoa—the very place the Lord sent him to preach the gospel so many years before. Given knew that since the Kondoa school system offered an inadequate education at best, going back there now would essentially mean no income. It would also mean that he and Lilian would have to live apart from their precious children once again. The Gaula children would almost certainly have to remain in Dodoma where an accredited international school could do a much better job of preparing them for the future.

A call for prayer went out once more to friends and supporters around the world. My husband and I were among those who prayed for the Lord to make his will known to both Given and Lilian. As a result of spending time in prayer over our friend's desire to hear from God, I was led to share Mordecai's words to his cousin, Hadassah (Esther). "And who knows but that you have come to your royal position for such a time as this?" (Esther

4:14b). This certainly seemed like fitting words for the Gaulas as they prepared to make a difficult decision.

I did not know it at the time, but other friends across the globe also quoted the same Scripture reference. The Holy Spirit was once again using a chorus of others to speak into the Gaulas' lives. "Every matter must be established by the testimony of two or three witnesses" (2 Corinthians 13:1b). The Anglican Diocese of Kondoa, in complete disarray at the time, was about to receive a new Bishop, one who would sweep the house clean and open wide its windows to the transforming winds of the Holy Spirit. Without looking back, the Gaula family made plans to return home to Tanzania, this time to Kondoa.

As the newly installed Bishop, Given no doubt looked around the diocese and saw a myriad of impossible challenges. Instead of giving in, he invited God to work through him to accomplish the impossible. Now the leader of his people, Given is first and foremost, a man of the people. "Many don't realize where I have come from," he says, "or that I am just like them." It is because he has worked so hard to turn his disadvantages into blessings that he is able to inspire hope in others and encourage them to work for a better future. Perhaps that is why he is so willing to share the details of his painful past now. "When others see that God never left my side, perhaps they will believe that God will do the same for them no matter what comes their way."

Think of the irony. God did not choose a person with sufficient means to carry out his grand plan for the people of Tanzania as one might expect. No! He selected a humble young man with absolutely no resources to his name except for an overwhelming desire to obey God. I can almost see a smile breaking across our Father's face those many years ago as he pointed to an unknown black child living in a remote village. "I choose you!" How marvelous to know that God delights in using the improbable to do the impossible. "God chose things the world considers foolish in order to shame those who think they are wise. And he chose things [and people] that are powerless to shame those who are powerful" (1 Corinthians 1:27, NLT).

NOTES

1. Gaula, *The Gospel of Luke as a Model for Mission in an African Context: With Special Reference to Challenges of Mission in the Anglican Church of Tanzania.*

2. Julius Nyerere governed Tanganyika as its Prime Minister from 1961 to 1963, its President from 1963 to 1964, and as President of Tanganyika's successors state, Tanzania, from 1964 to 1985. Nyerere used *ujamaa* to substantiate the need for reform among his people after the country won its independence from Britain in 1961. The Swahili word, *ujamaa*, describes a form of socialism in which people realize their potential through the people or community. In other words, *ujamaa* embraces the principles of cooperative economics in which local people cooperate to provide the essentials of living for the whole community. In 1967, President Nyerere published his development blueprint entitled, the "Arusha Declaration." *Arusha Declaration*, Wikipedia https://en.wikipedia.org/wiki/arusha_declaration (accessed February 14, 2016).

part two

MELINA

She is clothed with strength and dignity...
Proverbs 31:25a

6
A Woman of Grace

Her children arise and call her blessed

Proverbs 31:28a

From the moment the Holy Spirit first placed this writing assignment on my heart, I knew I had to interview Given's mother, Melina. I felt sure she would help me understand how her son had become such a devoted advocate for his people, including those who had treated him so badly. Having initially met Melina during my first trip to Tanzania in 2007, I was already aware that she had played a large part in her son's strong faith. His story would be incomplete without her input since she, more than any other person, instilled in him the absolute necessity for trusting God in every area of life.

The Bible has much to say about the role of godly women like Melina. In Paul's letter to Timothy, his faithful companion and devoted disciple, he said, "I am reminded of your sincere faith, which first lived in your grandmother Lois and in your mother Eunice and, I am persuaded, now lives in you also" (2 Timothy 1:5). In the same way, I believe that Melina's sincere faith lives on in her son, Given.

Mdala Melina Salwa was born into the Salwa clan of her parents in Lugala, Dodoma, on August 18, 1949. The third of ten children, she was one of only four daughters. In God's great providence, her family heard the gospel story for the first time during the great missionary period when the Church Mission Society began to make inroads into Tanganyika (later named "Tanzania") in the late 1920s.

When she reached an acceptable age to marry, Melina's parents insisted she look for a suitable partner outside the pagan community. Perhaps they wanted to give her every advantage for a successful marriage. Maybe they simply wanted to ensure a Christian lineage for their generations to come. Although they did not realize it at the time, their well-intentioned demands would set Melina on a collision course with evil.

Eventually, Melina met a young man named Viligio. Although his family converted from paganism to the Roman Catholic faith, her parents were not satisfied. They insisted that she and her husband-to-be attend an evangelical Anglican church. There was one problem, however. There were no Anglican churches in the area.

Audacious as it may sound, Melina made the bold decision to start the process for establishing a church soon after she and Viligio were married. She asked the presiding bishop to send a catechist (lay pastor) to conduct services. Never one to sit idly by, Melina went to each door inviting her neighbors to church. Before long, the entire village of 400 people accepted Christ as their personal Savior. Everyone except Viligio, that is. While he professed faith in Jesus, his life did not bear witness to any measure of spiritual transformation. He was an alcoholic who seemingly had no desire to change his ways.

The months and years brought only more misery for Melina as her husband sank ever deeper into a world of alcohol-fueled neglect. She desperately wanted to escape her own hell on earth, but she knew that if she tried, Viligio would refuse to let her take the boys with her. According to societal norms, children are considered a husband's property regardless of whether he wants, or is able to care for them. Even though Viligio's mother was the only person who ever showed Melina any kindness, she, too, would never condone her daughter-in-law's wish to leave. "I knew it was better for me to die with my children than to leave them to die alone," Melina says. "I still cry when I think about those days."

However, the persecution from her husband and his clan became so unbearable that in a weak moment, she made the terrible decision to run away. She stealthily made her way to the train station and boarded one of the cars knowing that it spelled freedom, albeit only temporary. Beyond that, she would not contemplate the future. For the moment at least, she was resolute. She would do whatever it took to find peace and security.

The train no sooner left the station than Melina was overcome with remorse and guilt. How could she ever have considered leaving her precious sons? Frantic, she knew she had to get off the train, even though by now it was moving at a good rate of speed. With every ounce of courage she could muster, she opened the door and jumped as far away as possible from the chugging, iron locomotive. "I could have died," she says, "but I thought only of my children in that moment." Bruised, but still able to walk, Melina returned home defeated.

Although her parents were either unable, or unwilling to help, her maternal grandmother did what she could to supply a little food from time to time. It wasn't much, but it kept them alive. Apart from her, no one came to her assistance. In his great mercy, God gave Melina the patience to persist during many years of unimaginable suffering. "I believe God was helping me to endure even though I had to watch my children suffer." Melina has long since forgiven her husband to whom she has remained faithful and continues to live with all these years. "Forgiveness and forgetfulness are two different things," she tells me. With eyes averted, and voice barely audible, she whispers that she will forever be haunted by the memory of her son hanging over the fire.

As Given translates his mother's story for me, I notice tears in her eyes and realize that I have seldom seen her smile. I find myself imagining her as a young child. Even though her family was poor, she must have joined the other village children as they laughed and sang and danced about. Surely her life wasn't all that bad. Or was it? Sadly, the innocence of childhood ended far too soon only to be replaced by the harsh realities of life. Today, her lined face and stiff movements cause her to look older than her actual years. Still, there is a grace and dignity about this woman that I respect and admire. I know that each time I return for a visit, I will be greeted with a rare smile and a kiss on each cheek. I love Melina. I do. Her life is a testimony to God's faithfulness, his providential care. In my estimation, she is a giant among women of the faith. If I am ever tempted to despair, I only have to think of her godly example.

There is one final question to ask Melina before the interview ends. "As you look at the past, do you see God's hand on your life and that of your son's?" Her answer comes quickly and without hesitation. "Yes. I marked every instance even then, and waited to see what the end result would be. I really wanted to know God's plan for my son. Looking back now," she says, "I see the purposes of God clearly."

I shake my head, and turning to Given, ask him to tell her that I hold her in the highest regard. "Tell her how very special she must be for God to have chosen her to suffer so for his sake." She seems a bit taken aback at such a statement. I imagine she never thought of herself in quite that way. She seems to want to say more, so I wait. "From an early age," she says, "I decided to follow God. He has caused my son to watch over me. If I am hungry, he provides for me. If I am sick, he makes sure I receive medical attention. He works hard to take care of me even today."

The same manner in which Melina protected her son as best she could for all those years, he now does the same for her. They join their prayers for the salvation of her other son and Given's brother, Michael, and his wife, both of whom are alcoholics. They pray for Michael's 7 children who range in age from 2 to 22 years. They also pray for Viligio. They will never give up because they know that with God, all things are possible, even Viligio's salvation.

Melina's voice suddenly grows faint, and I have to lean in closer to hear her parting words. "I know this book you are working on is God's work," she says unexpectedly. "It is God's miracle. Only he could unite people of different color, and cause them to be as brothers and sisters. It was God's eternal plan." She adds with a whisper, "You know where we come from. We are the poorest of the poor, and yet God has called you to love us. I thank God for choosing you to share our stories of his unending love." As I rise to kneel before her and kiss her dear hands, we both have tears in our eyes. Surely this is what Christ intended for his people when he told them to love one another *as I have loved you* (John 13:34). There is nothing I would not do for this woman. I hope she knows that.

part three

LILIAN

*Stories make us more alive, more human,
more courageous, more loving.*

Madeleine L'Engle

7

Humble Beginnings

*Your eyes saw my unformed body; all the days ordained for
me were written in your book before one of them
came to be.*

Psalm 139:16

Lilian Gaula and I sit together sipping tea while we munch on breakfast
leftovers—a few delicious Mandazi, the East African version of donuts,
and several fried spicy meat- and vegetable-filled Samosas purchased from
an Arab merchant in town. This is the first time since I arrived three weeks
ago that we have had a chance to relax and talk without interruption—
except for the constant ringing of a cell phone, that is.

In truth, there is never a time when calls are not being made, or received.
Unlike our first visit in 2007 when my husband and I rarely saw a cell phone,
today they are everywhere. Inexpensive phones shipped from China flood
the local markets before finding their way into the remotest of villages.
Although the phones break frequently, a new one can be purchased for only
a few Tanzania shillings. Some people, like the Bishop, often carry more

than one to ensure maximum service provider coverage. In this place where runners and bicyclists still travel miles to deliver messages, phones offer uncommon convenience and immediacy.

I understand this and am not disturbed when Lilian's phone rings yet again, and she steps into the other room to talk. I could allow myself to worry that I might never complete my interviews. However, I am keenly aware that even in this, God is in control. All things, including this interview, will be accomplished in his perfect (kairos) time. As Given often reminds anxious, clock-watching western visitors, "Things start when we get there." Indeed they do.

For the moment, I am content to enjoy a respite, however brief, from the usual activity of the Bishop's house. All is quiet except for the occasional crowing of a rooster and the happy sounds of young children playing in the dirt nearby. The women who walk up the hill from the village each day to help Lilian prepare meals when visitors are in town are nowhere to be seen. No doubt they are off shopping for produce, or a live chicken to sacrifice for the evening meal. It is not unusual to see a poor, unfortunate hen, or rooster spend its last hours tethered by the leg to a bush, or small tree, waiting for its inevitable demise.

Even though recent droughts have devastated local fields, more fertile regions continue to thrive and produce a bounty of fruits and vegetables to truck into the smaller villages. Despite the fact that locals have precious little money to spend on such tantalizing arrays of food, perusing the open-air market offers the women a pleasant respite from their otherwise harsh existence. Sturdy pots and pans, and a variety of wood and metal kitchen tools hang over tables mounded high with every kind of food imaginable. Voices of energetic hagglers and neighborly conversation can be heard at every turn.

Just the other day, I had time to enjoy a leisurely stroll through the narrow passageways of the Kondoa market with my brother, Frank, who was along for his first visit to Africa. We were amused to observe female vendors laughing with one another while their young children scampered about playing games and hiding behind their mothers' skirts. Muslim women, garbed in their modest coverings known as hijabs, easily conversed with those dressed in more traditional African kanga wraps. If only for a few hours, the desperate realities of their difficult lives were set aside for the sake of friendship and neighborly camaraderie.

Today, I wait patiently for Lilian to take her place on the sofa once more to open the book of her life that I know is filled with the unmistakable evidence of God's guiding hand. I am aware that she is not feeling well. I heard her coughing last night from my room down the hall where I tossed and turned until the dark of night finally gave way to the gray veil of early morning. My overactive mind wove a web of doubt that kept me awake far too long as I lay listening to the sounds of the night. Will Lilian be too ill to grant me this interview? Will I have enough material to fill a book-sized manuscript? There seemed to be no end to my list of "what if's." As usual, I worry in vain. I know Lilian is more than eager to share tales from her past. In fact, she has been looking forward to this as long as I have.

Over the years, Lilian has become the dearest of friends to me. It is truly amazing. Although our cultures and experiences are quite literally worlds apart, we often understand one another without having to say a word. Perhaps it is that special connection women share. Certainly, that's part of it, but I think it is also because God has knit our hearts together in such a special way. I know that only our Heavenly Father could make such a friendship possible. "Friends come and friends go, but a true friend sticks by you like family" (Proverbs 18:24, MSG). Our long friendship has shown that to be the case over and over again.

"I have many, many, many things to tell you about what God has done in my life; so many you can't imagine," Lilian says as she walks back into the room. I pick up my pen and paper, and turn on the recorder, eager to capture every word.

"My name is Lilian, Joseph (Mdahe) Jeremia (Malaya) Zakaria [Gaula], but my father's family always called me by my Cigogo name, Nyendo," she says. "Until four generations ago, it was uncommon to have a Christian name." She explains that the East Africa Revival changed

As in the Old Testament, a person's lineage is revealed in the patrilineal surnames of past generations. Christian (English) names are often adopted at baptism. Kinship is integral to community life. It regulates natural affinity, loyalties, obligations of relatives and even acceptable ways to relate to outsiders.[1]

everything as more and more people accepted English names at the time of their baptism.

Lilian came into the world January 8, 1966, the second of ten children born to Vailet and Joseph. Like most Tanzanians, her genealogy lays familial claim to a number of indigenous tribes. Her line includes ancestors from the Sukuma and Wagogo tribes, two of the many Bantu ethnic and linguistic groups of Tanzania.[2]

The Zakaria family line links to other tribes as well, such as the powerful, warring Hehe who expanded northward from the mountainous Iringa Region of south central Tanganyika during the infamous anti-colonial HeHe Rebellion of 1891.[3] Led by a violent and much-feared chief, the HeHe tribe indiscriminately pillaged, assaulted, and murdered Germans along with the local tribes living and working along the central caravan route. Among those killed were many Wagogo clan members. It is from their royal Gogo lineage on her mother's side that Lilian is descended.

My friend made her earthly entrance at the Mvumi Hospital, an Anglican-run healthcare facility whose mission was, and remains 50 years later, "to glorify God." I cannot help but think that even in choosing this hospital, God was declaring a course for this daughter "created in Christ Jesus to do good works, which God prepared in advance" for her to do (Ephesians 2:10). God had very special plans for Lilian. Only he knew that 24 years later to the day, she would walk through the doors of this same hospital to serve as its chaplain. Truly, "The Lord makes firm the steps of the one who delights in him" (Psalm 37:23). Lilian would need to remind herself of this in the years ahead as she found herself embroiled in a powerful and terrifying struggle between good and evil. Her first introduction came early as she watched her mother fall victim to malevolent spirits.

NOTES

1. Yusufu Turaki, Lausanne Movement, Lausanne.org (retrieved Mary 31, 2016).

2. The ethnic and linguistic Bantu group known as the Gogo based in the Dodoma Region, constituted the third largest tribal population in Tanganyika in the past. Its people were regarded as a conservative group that strictly adhered to its own tribal customs and traditions. Marriage outside of the tribe was frowned upon, if not forbidden, by family members.

3. Tanganyika was known as German East Africa until the end of the First World War that lasted from 1914 until 1918. When the German occupation ended, the British government was given a mandate over the region and subsequently named it Tanganyika Territory. David Livingstone's explorations did much to open Central Africa to the future work of the missionary, trader and settler. After Livingstone's death, missionaries bravely stepped in to take up where he left off. They willingly endured great hardship and loneliness in order to profess the name of Christ to many who had never heard his name.

8

My Mother,
the Medicine Woman

There is another world, but it is in this one.
William Butler Yeats, Irish Poet

A young mother sat alone in her darkened house. Except for the occasional crowing of a rooster, or the muffled conversation of people on their way to market, the only sounds she heard were the voices of relatives who had long since passed from this life to the next. The good spirits came to her in the early morning hours. They guided her deep into the forest to show her where to gather leaves and dig for roots to cure certain illnesses, or even to break a curse. Soon, more sinister voices began to trouble her dreams and eventually her waking hours. "If you do not do as we say," they threatened, "we will cause you to kill yourself."[1]

> The Bible warns believers that Satan and his demonic spirits sometimes masquerade as good spirits. For that reason, it is vital that we test the spirits to see whether they are of God (see 2 Corinthians 11:14 and 1 John 4:1-4).

For seven long years, Vailet descended into a dark world where few would wish to go. Her eldest daughter, Lilian, was forced to care for the other children while absorbing all the chores her mother left undone. At times, after walking home from school, the young girl heard multiple voices coming from behind the closed doors and windows of her mud house. Past experience taught her that when she walked through the door, she would find her mother alone, seated in her usual chair with a variety of strange-sounding, and often competing voices coming from her throat.

Sometimes the voices spoke in the Cigogo dialect of her tribe. At other times, they used the language of the Masai, or the Sukuma. As often as not, angry, commanding male voices spoke in Arabic as if arguing with the seemingly more benign female voices. These "spirits" told Vailet many things she could not have known, such as her daughter's conversation with classmates in which she detailed her mother's demonic possession. Though young, Lilian instinctively knew that evil spirits had taken over her mother. As time passed, Vailet grew increasingly oblivious to everything around her except the voices claiming to be her unseen ancestors.

"We want to give our granddaughter knowledge," the good voices would say to one another, "so that she can help our people." Vailet proved to be an excellent student adept at "divining" the cause of someone's misfortune before offering them a holistic remedy to restore harmonious order and balance.[2] However, when she tired of being told what to do, and she attempted to resist their control, the voices of the evil spirits began to drown out those of the more benevolent ones.

Attempting to make sense of such otherworldly interaction is uncomfortable at best for westerners today, but not so for traditional Africans. This is especially true for people living in sub-Saharan Africa who, like Vailet, view the visible and invisible worlds as inextricably intertwined. They are taught to believe that ancestors play a vital role in everyday life by connecting the natural world to the spirit world, and the past to the present. Within the context of African cosmology, ancestors often serve as mediators between those on earth and the "Supreme Being." Consequently, it is not unusual to hear accounts of dead relatives, otherwise known as the living dead, appearing before loved ones in dreams and visions to instruct, or bless them.[3]

Even knowing this, I can't imagine why Vailet's ancestors would wish to harm her. That is, until I learn that ancestors are known to declare curses on those who refuse to do as they say. I wonder if these spirits are actually demons masquerading as relatives, and if so, why are they allowed to exert such influence over the living? I am aware that Vailet attended church regularly before her nightmare began, but wonder if she had truly encountered Jesus as her personal Savior. What door did she leave open to allow the enemy to take up residence inside her? When I ask Lilian about this, she takes a deep breath, and prepares to tell me just how it was that the thief slipped in to steal, kill and destroy her mother (see John 10:10). I suspect that what I am about to hear will stretch the limits of my imagination, and most definitely exceed the boundaries of my own experience.

"It all began in 1977 when my father decided to go on holiday without my Mum," Lilian says. Joseph told his wife that he was going to Chinyika, the village where his parents lived some 75 kilometers away. Then he bought two small bags to pack what few clothes he had before setting out.

While he was gone, spirits came to Vailet in the night. "Your husband didn't go to Chinyika as he told you," they said. "He took a train to Zambia with another woman." Vailet wondered how this was possible since she knew of no trains going to Zambia. Sensing her doubt, the spirits told her that the Tazara (Tanzania/Zambia) Railway had recently been completed. Although she had no way of knowing it at the time, passenger travel service had been available for several months. Saying nothing, Vailet held these things in her heart until she could decide what to do.

Two days later, her sister-in-law came for an unexpected visit. "Is your brother in Chinyka with his family?" Vailet asked her. "No," came the answer. "Mdahe [Joseph] is not there." Now Vailet knew the spirits were telling her the truth. She was devastated. Her husband had always been a good, kind man, a hard working provider, and loving father. He had always been careful to abide by his father's advice to "never, ever in your life beat your wife." How could he betray her in this way now? She didn't hesitate to confront him with the truth when he returned. Lilian overheard part of their heated conversation. "It is better for you to beat me than what you are doing," her mother said.

After his deception was brought to light, Joseph no longer bothered to hide his relationship with the woman he now called his second wife. Vailet sank into a state of depression until, at last, she gave herself over to the total control of the dark spirits. "My father couldn't seem to stay away from this woman," Lilian explains. They even had several children together adding to the five she already had by another man.

Having good intentions, even if sadly misplaced, Mdahe did his best to provide for both families. If he spent money on Vailet and her children, he felt obligated to buy things for his other family, and vice versa. Although he had a good job with the government, his income was now divided between two families. As a result, Vailet was forced to make local beer to supplement their income. At one point, the spirits told her to stop making it.[4] When she refused to comply, they threatened to kill her youngest daughter, Pendo. Lilian could hear the voices of the good spirits pleading, "No. Please help our daughter. Don't do this to her. Help our daughter." It was 1979, and Lilian was only 13 years old.

In spite of the warnings, Vailet continued to make and sell her beer. One day, the baby suddenly became so ill that it seemed likely she would die. Realizing the spirits were making good their threat, Vailet frantically tossed out all her beer-making supplies, the flour, water, pots—everything. She even washed her body to remove all traces of her work. Almost immediately, baby Pendo began to improve. On some level, Vailet must have known her life was now firmly in the hands of her ancestors' spirits.

After a few years, another baby girl, Fromena, was born. Vailet was sinking ever deeper into the dark pit of demonic possession. The new baby refused to nurse, and soon became very thin. Even though young, Lilian stepped in to cook and care for her other siblings. With both father and mother abdicating their parental duties, life was very difficult and confusing for Lilian.

One night, the spirits whispered another evil secret to Vailet. "Your husband is under a spell," they said. "The woman wears an amulet in her bra to ensure her power over Mdahe." Each time she touches it and calls his name, he comes to her. The spirits told Vailet that if Mdahe went to the woman's house when she was not home, he would find the amulet in a bra she had hidden away. Lilian remembers hearing her mother tell him to look for the object, and to bring back whatever he found.[5]

Sure enough, he discovered the amulet exactly where the spirits said it would be. Lilian watched as her mother carefully untied the bag and took out its contents. There were several items inside, including a folded piece of paper with what looked like Arabic writing on it. "For some reason," Lilian says, "my mother didn't fear witchdoctors, and she quickly burned the paper." Then she told her husband, "Only one thing remains. Go again to your second wife's house, and make sure she is not home. Dig under the front door, and you will find a red root." Mdahe did as he was instructed, but instead of finding a red root, he found a red metal object that he took to Vailet. Lilian is not certain how her mother disposed of it, but she knows that she did. "Maybe she put it in the toilet."[6]

From that time on, Lilian's father believed what his wife was telling him. "It was not you," she assured him. "Because you are not strong, you were easily led by this woman who put a spell on you." Although Mdahe eventually stopped going to see the other woman, he continued to provide for their children. Still, Vailet remained under the control of the spirits. Lilian recalls her mother saying on more than one occasion that if she ever left the house in the morning and failed to return, Lilian was not to look for her. "If you do," she said, "you will find me dead."

One morning as Vailet left the house, Lilian sensed that something was unusual about this day. Even though fearing what she would find, she was compelled to follow her mother at a safe distance. To Lilian's astonishment, Vailet did not go deeper into the forest, but instead went to the home of a godly Masai pastor. Lilian quietly retraced her steps home. In the evening, her mother returned. Something was different about her, Lilian thought. "Bring my baby to me," she instructed when she saw Lilian with her youngest daughter nestled securely in a sling on her back. "From that day on, my mom began to laugh again," Lilian says. "She even began to sing a new song about the joy of the Lord." Lilian later learned that when her mother got to the home of the pastor, he and his wife prayed and fasted the entire day to break the spiritual stranglehold Satan had on Vailet. The result was that she was gloriously set free. She came home in her right mind for the first time in nine years.

"From this day," Vailet told her family, "you will never hear me talking with those demons again. Only the Holy Spirit will be talking to me now." Vailet returned to church, and even joined the choir. She sings in the same choir to this day.

Teacher, I brought you my son, who is possessed by a spirit that has robbed him of speech...I asked your disciples to drive out the spirit, but they could not..." he rebuked the impure spirit..."I command you, come out of him and never enter him again." After Jesus had gone indoors, his disciples asked him privately, 'Why couldn't we drive it out?' He replied, 'This kind can come out only by prayer.'

Mark 9:17b, 18b, 25, 28-29

NOTES

1. The supernatural world is thought to be full of spirits whose abodes include trees such as silk cotton, baobab, sycamore, and burial grounds, etc. Spirits are classified as being good or bad. Evil spirits are always associated with Satan. Africans, among others, practice exorcism, believe in life after death, future reward and future punishment. Kato, Byang H., *Theological Pitfalls in Africa*, (Evangel Publishing House, 1975, Nairobi, Kenya). p. 36-418.

2. Gaula, *The Gospel of Luke as a Model for Mission in an African Context: With Special Reference to Challenges of Mission in the Anglican Church of Tanzania*. p. 68. Many African Christians continue to practice their African Tribal Religion (ATR) in secret, particularly in a desperate search for healing. "They will first try medical clinics, but medication is expensive and limited. They will next ask the priest or evangelist to pray for them, but if they are not healed, the average, uneducated priest or evangelist will dismiss them, saying that they do not have enough faith! Thus, they feel their only alternative is to seek help in ATR, which many African Christians in Tanzania sadly consider more effective than Christianity."

3. The challenges of reflecting Christianity in the African cultural context are legion. Tanzanians, among others, practice inclusivism by merging Christianity with their own African Traditional Religions including witchcraft. Roman Catholic Cardinal Polycarp Pengo laments "the phenomenon common in many African societies of Christianity on Sunday mornings and the practice of witchcraft and sorcery during the rest of the week." *Africa: Why Belief in Witchcraft Remains Strong Among Africans*. Clerical Whispers. http://clericalwhispers. blogspot.co.nz/2009/04/africawhy-belief-in-witchcraft-remains.html (accessed April 9, 2016).

4. Local beer is made by soaking maize in water for a day before allowing it to sprout. It is then and taken to milling machines. The result is a product that works like yeast to aid the fermentation process.

5. "The manifestation and the use of the impersonal powers are related to the practices of medicine men and women, and seers who use natural objects, plants and animals for medicine, magic, charms and amulets. Some specialists believe that mysterious powers imbedded in things or objects can be extracted for specific uses. Mystical and mysterious powers can be transmitted through certain object media or by pure spiritual means. Mystical powers can be sent to specific destinations for an intended good or evil. Mystical powers can be contagious by contact with objects carrying or mediating such powers." Turaki, Yusufu, *Africa Traditional Religious System as Basis of Understanding Christian Spiritual Warfare*. www. lausanne.org/content/west-african-case-study.

6. In rural areas toilets are usually holes in the ground. When *squat toilets* are enclosed indoors, the holes are sometimes lined with porcelain or concrete.

9

Encounters
of Another Kind

Do not forget to show hospitality to strangers, for by
so doing some people have shown hospitality to angels
without knowing it.

Hebrews 13:2

"I must tell you about a dream I had a very long time ago after my mother was delivered from the enemy's control," Lilian tells me. "God came to our house wearing a long white robe like men do in the Middle East today." I'm sure I must have raised an eyebrow when she stated so emphatically that it was God who came to visit. The man did not appear to be in a hurry, she told me, but chose to stay quite awhile. "Talk, talk, talk," she adds. I have learned that when Tanzanians want to add emphasis to what they are saying, they often repeat a word, or phrase several times. Clearly, this stranger spent a great deal of time chatting with both mother and daughter. After awhile he got up to leave, and Lilian and Vailet walked him to the edge of their village. Although Lilian didn't understand the significance of the strange visit at the time, she later came to believe that it was God's messenger sent in advance of her call to the ministry.

The following year, 1984, a terrible famine spread across the land. "Sometimes we would go three days without eating anything," Lilian says softly. To alleviate such widespread suffering, government officials trucked in bags of red millet, the kind normally used to make beer. It wasn't what they were used to eating, but it was edible enough when ground into flour for the stiff porridge known as *ugali* (*wugali*).

One day, while Lilian was outside helping her mother cook the porridge over hot coals, an old man appeared. One minute he wasn't there, and the next he was. Unlike the man in Lilian's dream a year earlier, this older, but very real man came with a special request having to do with the bag of red flour he carried under one arm. She remembers that he was very dirty. "I have walked a long way trying to find someone to cook for me," he said. "Each time I stop to ask for help, I am chased away. Please, won't you make me some *ugali*? Then I will go." Although they were already cooking *ugali* using this same kind of flour, the man insisted he would only eat that which was made from his flour.

"Where do you come from, old man?" my mother asked. "I have come from Handari," he replied. Lilian had never heard of such a place. "Handari is very dry," he explains. "We have not seen rain for three years, and I am very hungry." As Vailet set about cooking a separate pot of porridge using the man's flour as requested, she told her daughter to go ahead and eat what had already been prepared. "We were so hungry," Lilian recalls. "Although I wanted to wait, I couldn't." When the man's food was ready, he only ate a little of it. "I am hungry," he said, "but I can't eat a very big amount." When he tried to leave the remaining flour with them, Vailet insisted he take it home for later use.

"Where are you going now?" Vailet asked the old man as he rose to leave. "I am going to see my friend in the village of Vinghawe." When he mentioned the name of his friend, Vailet realized she knew this person. "We will escort you there," she announced. And so the three of them set off together for Vinghowe. When they got close to the village, the old man told them to leave him there. He would walk the rest of the way by himself. He blessed them, and thanked them for their kindness. "You have a good heart even though you don't know me." Then he pronounced a special blessing on Vailet's parents and grandparents as well.

As Lilian finishes relating this story, she smiles. "Do you want to hear something strange?" she asks. "Fourteen years later, Handari was the first parish Given and I were sent to shepherd." It was immediately clear to me that the visits from these two men, one in a dream, and one in the flesh, were somehow significant. I thought for a moment before replying. "Lilian, I believe God was letting you know that Handari was hungry for God, and had been without anyone to tell them of Jesus' love." Lilian nodded. "I think that is the right interpretation."

Lilian and I continue to talk, and I begin to see a larger picture. "I feel the Holy Spirit may have asked others to feed his sheep in Handari, but they refused," I tell her. "You were the only one who said, 'yes.'" A verse in Isaiah came to mind: "Then I heard the voice of the Lord saying, 'Whom shall I send? And who will go for us?' And I said, 'Here am I. Send me!'" (Isaiah 6:8).

God has always communicated with Lilian in special ways even when she was very young. In fact, a number of people gave her early clues about her future work for the Lord that only hindsight would make clear to her. For instance, when she was about 10 years old, she was walking to her school in Chinyika when she came across an old man who, unknown to her, had once been a church catechist. He seemed to know her. "Come," he called to her using her clan name. Then he took her by the hand and led her to the old church cemetery. "Here is where your ancestor is resting," he said. Then he left.

"I didn't know until that moment that any of my ancestors were buried there on the church grounds." In 2012, Lilian returned to Chinyika to find the old man still alive. She told him that she was now a pastor like her paternal four times great grandfather who was buried there. Lilian tells me that she was the first minister to come from her clan. She was also the first woman to ever be ordained.

Even though Lilian made her own personal decision to follow Christ after her mother's remarkable deliverance, she continued to struggle with understanding how to view the values of her African traditional belief system in light of her newfound faith. One issue in particular presented her with a troubling dilemma. How did the notion of the *mizimu*, the living dead, line up with Scripture? Was it actually possible for some diabolical alchemy to transform dead people into creatures who walked among the living? Lilian would have to answer this for herself in the not too distant future.

10
Voices in the Night

*A third time the Lord called, 'Samuel!' And Samuel got up
and went to Eli and said, 'Here I am; you called me.'*

1 Samuel 3:8

Vailet and her family became regular church attendees following her miraculous deliverance. One Sunday, the minister, Rev. Kutoka, stopped Lilian after service to ask her to wait for him in his office. He told her that he had something he wanted to say to her. She was very afraid because she thought she had done something wrong. "I will be punished by God in front of that man of God," she thought. With great fear she walked down the hall and stood trembling outside the pastor's door.

"I believe that God is calling you," he said after joining her and inviting her in to his office. "I want to send you to Bible School." This certainly wasn't what Lilian expected. Although greatly relieved she was not in trouble, she didn't understand. She had just completed primary school, and had no hope of advancing to secondary school. Now her pastor was saying she should go to something called, "Bible School." What was a Bible School? The minister saw her questioning look, so he explained that she could learn more about God and his ways in this kind of school. "Go and talk to your mother and father about this," he told her, "and have them pay me a visit."

Delighted that their daughter was being offered such an opportunity, her parents went the very next day to see the Masai pastor lovingly referred to as Babu (grandfather). When Rev. Kukoka looked up to see Vailet walking in, he was shocked. This was the same woman he and his wife spent an entire day fasting for and praying that she would be delivered from demonic possession! Was her healing part of a bigger picture, one that would impact her own daughter? He felt sure it was, but set the thought aside to talk about Lilian's future. After much discussion, they all agreed that Lilian would go to live and study at the Chamhawi Bible School later that same year.

One night, as Lilian was asleep in a dormitory room where 12 girls shared beds, she suddenly woke up to a voice. Someone had called her name. "Lilian..." Thinking her friend beside her had called out in her sleep, she reached over to touch her arm. "Cecilia, did you call me?" she asked. "No. Go back to sleep," came the muffled reply. She knew she hadn't been dreaming, but if Cecilia hadn't called her, who had? She looked around the room, but all the girls were fast asleep. Eventually, she, too, fell into a deep sleep.

Once more, the voice came. "Lilian..." Waking up with a start yet again, she had a terrifying thought. Had the living dead come to claim her, and take her back to their dark place of abode? Wanting more than anything to pull the covers over her head, she knew she couldn't. She simply had to find out who was calling her. She quietly tiptoed into the next room, but found that no one was awake there either. Now she was really frightened. Lilian hurried back to her bed. Although terrified, she was quite tired by this time, and soon fell into a deep sleep again.

The voice came a third time. "Lilian..." She opened her eyes, but still no one was moving about. Then she remembered hearing the Old Testament story of how God called to Samuel during the night. When the young boy ran to inquire of Eli, his mentor, he was told, "I did not call; go back and lie down." Samuel went into his master a second, and then a third time. Eli realized the Lord was calling the boy. "Go and lie down, and if he calls you, say, 'Speak, LORD, for Your servant is listening'" (1 Samuel 3:5b; 9a, NIV). Feeling somewhat comforted that it might be God and not the *mizimu* as she first feared, Lilian began to question if God likewise had a special purpose for her yet to be revealed.

As Lilian is relating this story, I remember that when I was a child my siblings and I would play the game of "Zombie." We understood that these were only make-believe creatures we imitated to scare each other as we ran around in the backyard at dusk. This, however, is not a game to Africans, even today. In 2007, during our first trip to Tanzania, my husband and I visited the home of a village pastor. As we sat around a low table eating rice and chicken, a young toddler wandered into the room. He took one look at us and ran shrieking out into the yard with his mother doing her best to catch him. We asked what had just happened. It seems that upon seeing our pale skin, the child assumed we were dead beings come to take him away. Poor child! I only hope he wasn't scarred for life.

I ask Lilian to tell me more about the role the living dead play today. "People continue to take advantage of the African belief in the living dead, but in a different way," she explains. "Sometimes wicked people use witchcraft to make loved ones believe their relatives are really dead when they are not. People see them walking about, and are deceived into thinking they are looking at a dead person when, in truth, what they are seeing is only a piece of wood, or some other object." They weep and mourn not knowing that their relatives or friends were kidnapped, given drugs to confuse them, and made to work as slaves.

In rare instances, these poor souls find a way to escape and return home only to be greeted by disbelieving family members. "I saw one myself," Lilian admits. "A wicked man abducted many people over the years to perform hard labor for him." When the man eventually died, and there was no one to keep them drugged, many came to their senses and ran away. "The man I saw was eventually stopped by people who caught him wandering around as if in a daze. They took him to the hospital in Mpapwa for evaluation." The villagers were shocked, as you might imagine, she explains. "They thought he had died 12 years before. In fact, they witnessed his burial," she adds. Or, so they thought. Soon after he was taken into slavery, his cruel master cut out his tongue so that he could not speak clearly. Somehow, the poor soul managed to convey the truth to his rescuers. He explained that he and others had been kept in a drug-induced state to erase every trace of their lives before they were kidnapped. To verify his claims, the police went to what they thought was his gravesite to see if they could dig up a body. All they uncovered were pieces of very old wood.

Lilian is reminded of another story about one of her aunts who lost her daughter. Although the aunt eventually became a Christian, she continued to believe in the living dead. "My aunt told me that her daughter, Gilita, came to her every night, knocking, knocking, knocking on her door." The mother would cry out in fear, "You are dead now. You have to know that. Don't come here anymore. We don't want you to come anymore."

"Just today," Lilian adds, "I saw a news report about a woman named, Neema, who came home after reportedly dying three years before. And just last year a boy who was thought to have died in Moshi, was found cutting timber in the forest." Although Lilian was well aware of such strange occurrences, she still didn't know what to make of them. "I didn't really believe them, but when I was attending St. Philip's Theological College, I studied with a pastor who used to be a witch doctor." He explained that whether people like it or not, witchcraft is a very real and powerful tool of the enemy. "Our people are not surprised, then, when we tell them about the resurrection of Jesus," Lilian says.

As strange as it sounds, belief in the living dead gives Africans a starting point for accepting the truth of Christ's death and resurrection. "We tell people that in some instances, loved ones and neighbors thought to be dead, may actually still be alive," Lilian explains. "The day will come, however, when they really will die. Christ, on the other hand, actually did rise from the dead never to die again." Lilian is quiet for a moment, and then says with emphasis, "Only God has the power to overcome such sorcery. Our people must hear this good news! We must tell them."

In his article featured in *Christianity Today* in 2016, Andrew Byers says that every deception and lie Satan can conceive "explodes on the cross of the One who bore the brunt of unspeakable disaster. But as the empty tomb makes clear, even that is not enough to ungift divine love."[1] How marvelous that nothing, human or otherwise, will ever stand in the way of God's redemptive plan to rescue, redeem, and restore fallen humankind.

NOTES

1. Byers, Andrew. "When God Is Strange and Awful." *Christianity Today*, June 2016, p. 75.

11
The Djinn

For our struggle is not against flesh and blood, but against the rulers, against the authorities, against the powers of this dark world and against the spiritual forces of evil in the heavenly realms.

Ephesians 6:12

One summer, while Lilian was on break from her studies at St. Philips Theological School, her friend, Maria, offered to let her stay at her house. As is often the case, the toilet was located in the back yard some distance from the house. Maria was careful to tell Lilian not to go outside at night to visit the toilet, but instead to use a pot that she would give her to keep in her room for emergency nighttime "short calls."

Certain she would not wake up during the night, for she rarely did, Lilian assured her friend that she would not be requiring the pot. At the time, another friend, Hilda, was also staying in the room with Lilian at the back of the house. Sometime during the night, Lilian woke up feeling like she would burst if she didn't go outside to use the toilet. "Hilda," she said as she shook her friend. "I can't sleep. I must go outside. Please go with me," she pleaded. "No," came the response. "We were told never to go outside at night." Lilian knew she couldn't wait. She would just have to go by herself. After all, it wasn't that far from the house. She quietly opened the back door where she noticed a high wall separating her friend's house from the one next door. Tall stalks of sugar cane were growing up against the wall. All of a sudden, she heard something that sounded like loud scratching. Thinking it might be a harmless cat sharpening its nails on the thick canes, she walked on towards the toilet. Without warning, three cats jumped to the top of the wall. They turned in unison to get a closer look at her.

I glance up from my notes to see Lilian trying to gauge my reaction. "They moved with precision almost as one," she emphasizes. According to Lilian, they were the largest cats she had ever seen. "In fact," she says, "they were almost as big as lions. Even their whiskers and tails were unusually long." One thing is for certain; these were no ordinary cats. Whatever they were, they were big enough to stop Lilian in her tracks, leaving her terrified to make a move. Something caught their attention causing them to focus beyond Lilian. In one perfectly synchronized turn, they gave her their backs. With that, she ran to the toilet, and quickly shut the door. She was determined to spend the rest of the night there. Then she thought, "I will call on the name of Jesus." Timidly she opened the door, and loudly proclaimed, "Jesus!" As she did, the cats jumped over the wall and left.

The next morning, when telling Maria what had taken place the night before, her friend explained that sometimes *djinn* appear in the form of cats.[1] "You know, our neighbor just beyond the wall is a witch [warlock]," Maria said. "Those particular *djinns* must belong to him." "People in the west do not like to hear these kinds of stories," Lilian tells me. "I understand they are frightened, but I want them to know that these things don't have any real power over those who believe in Jesus Christ."

Some years after she was first married, and Given was still in the States attending seminary, Lilian joined her children in Dodoma for several days. She had to take care of personal business at the bank in town, so she waited until the children left for school one day before boarding the bus (*dara dara*) into town. When she got to the bank, she joined the queue waiting to see one of the tellers. Before long, she noticed a very tall woman getting in line behind her. "She was very, very beautiful," Lilian says, "and taller than anyone I had ever seen." Interestingly enough, no one seemed to notice the woman. "Maybe I was the only one who could see her," Lilian suggests. As she continued to sneak quick looks at this most intriguing female, the woman's face began to change. Lilian had the distinct impression that she was very angry with her for staring, even though she was pretty sure she had not been caught.

Soon, other people joined the line, but rather than stepping behind the woman, they took their place in front of her. This puzzled Lilian. Why would she allow people to get ahead of her? All of a sudden, the woman looked directly into Lilian's eyes. With what sounded like a hissing sound, she abruptly turned to leave the bank, and instantly she disappeared. The door of the bank never opened. One minute she was there, and the next she was not.

Still perplexed, Lilian completed her transactions and went home thinking about what she had seen. She felt she had to share her experience with someone, so she went to see her friend, Maria, at Msalato Bible School. "Today I have seen a very tall and very beautiful lady," she told her friend. No sooner were the words out of her mouth than her friend announced, "It was a demon." Lilian was shocked. "What?" she said. "It was a demon," her friend repeated with complete certainty.

Lilian was greatly troubled, but wondered if her friend might be right. "Lord," she prayed, "if this is true, please let her return to the bank the next time I am there so I will know for sure." And then she added, "And please let her appear in a different form this time." Without realizing it, Lilian intuitively obeyed the command given to all believers. "Dear friends, do not believe every spirit, but test the spirits to see whether they are from God" (1 John 4:1a, NIV). She had made her request to God in faith believing that he would answer. He did.

A few days later, Lilian had reason to go back to the bank. When she opened the door, she saw an old woman sitting inside counting papers like one would count paper money. Once again, no one seemed to notice anything out of the ordinary except Lilian who couldn't imagine why the bank employees would let such a dirty woman sit inside the bank like that. With a flash of spiritual insight, Lilian suddenly knew this was the same lady she had seen earlier. God had answered her request to the letter. Rather than the tall, elegant lady she encountered the first time, this person was older, shorter, and filthy. Somehow Lilian knew that this was not a human, but something all together different. It was a *djinn*.[2]

After leaving the bank, Lilian walked to the town square where she spent several pleasurable hours purchasing vegetables and household items from the various vendors stationed on either side of the dirt road. When she finished shopping, she left the market to make her way to the bus station. As she approached the bus station, however, the same dirty, old woman suddenly appeared behind her. "Stop in the name of Jesus!" Lilian called loudly as she whipped around to confront the being. With that, the woman turned, and instantly disappeared. Lilian never saw either the young woman, or the old hag ever again.

This story has reminded Lilian of yet another encounter she had with *djinn* after Given took over as the new Bishop of Kondoa. He was away for a few days on church business, and since they could ill afford to hire a nighttime guard for the Bishop's residence, she always asked a friend, or relative to stay with her. On this particular occasion, she asked her niece, Debora, to keep her company. Since she didn't need to prepare the usual meals, she decided to fast for three days.

On the third day, Lilian was in her room praying late into the night. Some hours after retiring, the younger woman awoke to the sound of stray cats making a terrible racket nearby. About the same time, she heard Lilian praying. Her voice just kept getting louder and louder. The more Lilian prayed, the quieter the cats got until at last, they were silent. Debora got out of bed, and tiptoed into her aunt's room. "You know, Auntie," she said, "I heard you praying. Why did those cats stop crying when you prayed?" Knowing her niece was unaware that Kondoa had a very strong presence of witchcraft, she took time to explain that some people believe *djinn* can appear in the form of cats in order to carry out their evil plans.

When it came time for Debora to go home, Lilian walked her into town to catch an early morning bus back to Dodoma. After the bus left, Lilian realized she would have to walk home in the dark by herself. She hadn't thought of that until this moment. "What am I going to do?" She knew there were no houses around. In fact, much of the path wound through dense forest. "I was very afraid," she confesses, "but mostly about people who might be up to no good in the dark." Lilian prayed for protection, and began to make the return trip home.

"I felt as if I was a very big person walking with a very heavy step," she says. All of a sudden, she noticed a young man walking towards her, but when he saw her, he ran away. "God must have made me appear as a very big and very strong person to him so that he would not attack me," she says. "God showed me that even when Given is away, I don't have to fear anything."

Today Lilian knows how to place her trust in God even while living among practitioners of the dark arts. For example, it is a well-known fact that many sheiks are involved in witchcraft, and for that reason, are greatly feared. Yet, they always find a warm welcome in the Gaula household. "You know," Lilian says, "the sheiks mistakenly believe the Bishop and our Christian pastors are involved in witchcraft because their prayers bring results. They respect the Bishop out of fear, and even if we leave things outside our house unattended, they will not come to steal from us like they do others," she adds. "In a strange turn of events, the witchcraft-practicing sheiks are more afraid of the priests than they are of each other."

The Lord is with me; I will not be afraid.
What can mere mortals do to me?
Psalm 118:6

NOTES

1. African Muslims in particular believe in djinns—evil spirits of nature that are capable of shape shifting into many forms, human and otherwise.

2. According to modern lore, djinn encounters occur everywhere, and may be interpreted as other entities rather than their true selves. This is especially true of regions where little is known about them. Encounters with angels, fairies, demons, elementals [a magical entity who embodies, or personifies a force of nature], extraterrestrials, mysterious creatures, and ghosts of the dead may all be djinn in disguise, either playing tricks. or carrying out some other agenda. *If You Fear One Thing in Your Life, Fear The Djinn. The Greatest Masquerade of All: The Djinn*, Djinn Universe. www.djinnuniverse.com (accessed June 16, 2016).

12
Pennies from Heaven
...and More

And my God will meet all your needs according to the riches of his glory in Christ Jesus.

Philippians 4:19

L ilian longed to feel God's presence more than ever when her family faced a time of great uncertainty after moving to the strange new land of New Zealand with its unfamiliar multi-ethnic society. She was most troubled by the fact that her children had a difficult time making new friends since they had not yet learned to speak English. Now they were being thrust into a school system where they couldn't understand what anyone was saying, and no one could understand them. To help make their transition a bit smoother, Lilian asked to be allowed to sit in their classrooms to help translate lessons. Each day, as she watched her children sitting by themselves outside during the lunch hour, her heart would break. "I felt very, very sad," she says. "Mama, we don't have any friends," they told her. "We want to go home." Lilian wanted to return to Tanzania, too, but that wasn't an option. Thankfully, it wasn't long before the children began to learn English and make friends. When they no longer needed her assistance at school, Lilian looked for ways to pass the long days until the children came home. Still, she grew lonelier and lonelier. Most afternoons found her kneeling by her bed weeping. One day she heard a clear voice say to her, "You are a very stupid woman. Why are you crying? Why don't you pray to me so that I can provide what you want?"

"Yes, Lord," she admitted. "I am a very stupid woman. I feel so alone. Please help me." She tried sitting at the computer, cleaning the house, or quietly reading her Bible. Without her family's voices to fill the air, even the smallest of sounds seemed to echo through the empty house. One day, when Given and the children were at their respective schools, Lilian thought she heard movement. "Who is walking around my house?" she called out. She wondered if Given had forgotten something, and had come home to retrieve it. When she searched the house, however, no one was there. The same thing happened the next day and each day afterwards. In fact, she began to sense someone following her wherever she went. "Who is there?" she would shout. "Who are you, and why are you following me?"

One day she heard a very gentle voice in response to her questions. "Have you forgotten what you asked?" In an instant, Lilian remembered her request to the Lord, and as she did, Joshua 1:9 came to mind. "The Lord your God will be with you wherever you go." The voice said, "That is why I am following you." Then Lilian understood, and was greatly comforted. "Thank you, Lord," she said. "Thank you. Thank you." God had, indeed, answered the prayer of her heart. Now she knew for certain that God's presence was with her.

Still, she longed for people to share her days. "Lord, I need to have many, many people in my house like I do in Tanzania." All too soon Lilian would have reason to wish she had set a few parameters around her request. Although she eventually forgot her prayer, God did not, and just one year later, the Gaula household was overflowing with endless streams of visitors. The children invited new friends to their house. After awhile, their friends brought their parents to meet Lilian and Given. Sometimes Lilian's acquaintances asked her to watch their children while they went to work, or shopped. Yes. Her house was filled with people, just as it had always been in Tanzania.

On one particular Sunday, shortly after returning home from church, Lilian heard a knock at the front door. "Don't open it," she whispered to the children. "We are tired, and today we just need to be by ourselves." Then she heard a voice admonishing her. "Have you already forgotten what you asked me to provide?" Chastened, she hurried to open the door to a friend. After a lovely afternoon spent with sipping tea and conversing with her friend, Lilian felt totally refreshed. She was very glad she had not bolted the door after all. "Take delight in the LORD, and he will give you the desires of your heart.... . For great is his love toward us, and the faithfulness of the LORD endures forever. Praise the Lord" (Psalm 37:4; 117:2).

Every Sunday morning, Given left for church before Lilian and the children. "He said we took too long to get ready." She didn't mind, though. She enjoyed strolling along the streets lined with the lovely homes and beautiful gardens. On the return trip home, she and the children always stopped at the produce market to buy fruit for school lunches. She remembers one special Sunday when the minister preached from Malachi 3:8. "Will a mere mortal rob God? Yet you rob me. But you ask, 'How are we robbing you? "In tithes and offerings.'" Lilian distinctly heard the words, "Test me in this...and see if I will not throw open the floodgates of heaven and pour out so much blessing that there will not be room enough to store it" (Malachi 3:10).

She wondered at this as she waited for the ushers to pass the offering plate down each row of pews. However, on this day, the pastor told everyone to walk to the front of the church and place their tithes and offerings in the plates on the table before him. Lilian did not hesitate. She put the little amount of money she had set aside for fruit in the offering plate. "I felt very peaceful," she says. "I was very happy."

Unconcerned, Lilian passed by the market on the way home without stopping. The children wanted to know why. "I have given God your money," she said. Then with a smile added, "Sorry." The children didn't say a word as they continued to walk through the residential area. Lilian took notice of several bags placed on the sidewalk in front of a row of houses. It was not unusual for people to put items along the street for passersby to take what they wanted before the trash collectors came on Monday. Lilian couldn't help but see that beside one bag in particular, there were a number of purses strewn carelessly about, almost as if someone had gone through the lot and discarded the least desirable ones. "Oh, these are good handbags," she said to her children. "Maybe I will choose some." So she picked out two she especially liked, and happily carried them home.

Later that afternoon, Lilian set about cleaning out the purses. Inside the first one she found cloth handkerchiefs, tubes of lipstick, small mirrors, and flashlights. Then she opened the second purse to see that it was lined with a number of smaller interior pockets. She saw nothing of interest until she spotted a plastic bag filled with paper money bills.

Instead of New Zealand *kiwis*, however, it contained several denominations of Australian dollars. "What is this?" she thought guessing there might be as much as $50 Australian dollars inside. However, when she counted it all, she was surprised to find much more. "I have given God $10, and now I have found $300." Lilian was eager to share her news with Given, and together they carefully counted all the bills. It was certainly a lot of money. This had to be a mistake. Surely the woman who owned these purses did not realize that she had left money inside one of them.

"God, you can't give me this much money," Lilian whispered. "It is more than I gave you." She was determined to return the money to its rightful owner, if she could only find out who that was. Lilian returned to the exact place where she first discovered the bags, but no one was around. Lacking the time, or courage, to knock on each of the doors, she turned around to go home. "Maybe my friends can give me some advice," she thought. "Spend it," they each said when asked. "It's a gift from God." Still, she couldn't bring herself to do that, so she simply set it aside.

After some weeks passed, Lilian decided that perhaps her friends were right. She would take the money to the bank to change into *kiwis*. To her surprise, the exchange rate actually netted her $380.00 (equivalent to approximately US $218). "I will give 10 percent to the church," she reasoned. The rest she would set aside for the children's schooling.

One day she heard the sad news that her brother's wife had died giving birth to a baby girl. The child was named "Wema," which means "goodness." According to the custom of the land, since Lilian's brother had not given a dowry to his deceased wife's parents, they would take custody of the children. Lilian and Given discussed how they might help. "I know," Given said. "Let's give $100 to your brother so that he can pay his in-laws the bride price. "Then, if he can no longer care for the children by himself, they can come to live with us when we return to Tanzania."

As Lilian recounts this story, I realize that I had met Wema who was now a young woman. She was actually staying in the Gaula home in Kondoa during her summer break from school. "That money accomplished a lot, didn't it?" I ask. Lilian nods. "Yes. It actually served as a faith multiplier for our children, too. Now they want to give everything they have to the church," she adds with a laugh. "We have to counsel them to be wise with their money, and not give expecting to receive something in return."

Shortly before completing his doctoral program, Given received the unexpected news that the people of Kondoa wanted him to be their new bishop. They agreed that although they didn't want to accept, they hadn't followed God this far only to ignore his call, even if it was to something far different than initially planned. Given didn't seem to be worried, but Lilian was. She knew that the remote region was under the influence of demonic spirits. They decided to call in reinforcements, including their British expatriate friends living in New Zealand, to help them pray. They added a retired priest and his wife to a growing circle of intercessors.

As they gathered together one evening to unite in earnest prayer, the priest's wife saw a vision of a scorpion. Just as it was about to sting someone she couldn't quite identify, a shoe appeared out of nowhere, and crushed the predatory arachnid. What she saw next was even more surprising—a very large eye. The woman found it difficult to describe since she had never seen anything like it. It wasn't quite human, but it was not animal either. This sounded strangely similar to the story Lilian shared about a vision her sister, Wilice, had seen earlier. It, too, involved an eye, but as she looked intently at it, she saw Lilian and Given inside.

I couldn't get these images out of my mind, so I went online to try to find something that might be close to what both women had seen. When I showed Lilian a NASA image of the Helix Nebula called the "Eye of God," she immediately said, "Yes. I believe that is similar to what they described." (See appendix.)

A third confirmation about their call came the day Lilian and Given were taking a bus to New Plymouth, New Zealand. The whole time they were traveling, Lilian saw eyes like those of a lion in front of the vehicle staring directly at them. These eyes, unlike the others, were shining like the moon. Strangely enough, Lilian was not afraid. "Sometimes when I am tempted to doubt that God is with us," she says, "I remember each of these times that he showed us otherwise. I know no matter how I feel, I should never doubt that he is watching over us."

There was yet one more incident to relate. This one came in 2012 at Given's consecration as the new Bishop of Kondoa. At one point in the elaborate ceremony, a government regional commissioner stood behind the podium to deliver her speech. She turned to Given who was sitting on the dais, and said in strong, prophetic voice, "You servant of God; wherever you go, you must know that God's eye is seeing you."

Lilian was amazed and immediately thought about her friend's vision of God's eye in New Zealand, her sister's vision of the couple inside God's eye, her own vision of the eyes in front of the bus, and now this pointed reference to God's eye. He certainly was making sure they knew that he would never leave them nor forsake them no matter where he sent them to serve.

For the eyes of the Lord range throughout the earth to strengthen those whose hearts are fully committed to him.
2 Chronicles 16:9a

part four

VAILET

With man this is impossible,
but with God all things are possible.

Mark 19:26

13
Divine Destiny

In their hearts humans plan their course,
but the Lord establishes their steps.

Proverbs 16:9

M y time here in Africa is quickly drawing to a close, and only God knows if I will be able to return next year. There is but one final interview left to conduct before heading home. This one with Lilian's mother is non-negotiable, because without it, the chronicle of God's divine hand at work in this land would be lacking. I am keenly aware there are others I could include, but these are the stories I am meant to share here. I am certain of it.

Vailet has traveled three hours by bus from her village to be with me today, the last day of my visit. Having heard her stories long before meeting her for the first time in 2012, at her son-in-law's consecration as Bishop of

Kondoa, I saw her as living proof that Christ works in miraculous ways to push back the powers of darkness. Africans, in particular, are sorely in need of such a redemptive message, for without God's intervention, they continue to live as slaves to the enemy of their souls. As two veteran missionaries to Africa, Joseph Healey and Donald Sybertz explain, "Any theology that does not portray Jesus Christ as an all-powerful savior who here and now can free people from all fear, especially the fear of witchcraft and superstition, is inadequate. If Christianity means anything, it means freedom from fear of all kinds of oppression."[1] I believe that as well. Confirmation is found in God's Word. "So if the Son sets you free, you will be free indeed" (John 8:36).

We begin the interview with Vailet asking for God's blessing. "*Tuombe,*" she says. "Let us pray." With that call to prayer, her voice rises in gratitude to the God who has allowed her to live long enough to share her story for his eternal purposes. Her face radiates with the unmistakable conviction that she is a redeemed, cherished daughter of *El Elyon*, the God Most High. She is ready to open her heart and relive her difficult journey of the past.

Vailet was born sometime during the latter part of 1946. She doesn't know the exact month or day because many people could not read or write in those days. Her parents were no exception. Consequently, most could not keep accurate records for such things as birth and death. Parents remembered the year and season their children were born based on whether it was planting or harvesting time. Vailet is not even sure if she was the eleventh or twelfth of 16 children. Like so many other women without proper medical care, her mother had lost a number of babies through miscarriage, or early death. All together, she lost 12 children. Most succumbed to disease, including four sets of twins. Five children lived into adulthood. Out of those, only four are still alive today.

"I was named Nyamiti Uhile Mpina," Vailet says. "Mpina is my Sukuma tribal name, although it is usually given to a boy who has lost his father." It seems to me that Vailet was, indeed, a spiritual orphan until she found Christ. So perhaps the name is fitting after all. I believe I see other connections as well. For instance, Vailet's mother consulted a local doctor who gave her medicine to drink that would allow her to conceive. Her first name, *Nyamiti*, means "medicine girl." This seems especially prophetic since Vailet later became a local practitioner of sorts prescribing medicinal remedies for barrenness, among other maladies. Lilian was also called *Nyamati* because her mother took a liquid remedy to conceive her. In turn, Lilian did the same to prevent miscarrying her firstborn, Ihewa.

Evidence of violence runs through Vailet's bloodline. In the early days of civil war, as colonials advanced in the region, there was sporadic fighting between the HeHe people and the Nyamwezi, and also with the Sukuma. One of the more interesting stories of Vailet's ancestors is that of a Wahehe warrior who killed the Sukuma husband of a woman he desired. Sound familiar? His ultimate goal was to impregnate her so that her child would be raised as a HeHe. Sounds barbaric, but it was not unusual in those days.

"When I was a young girl," Vailet says, "my parents told me to sit on a very big log making noise to chase away the bugs munching on the millet." As unusual as it may sound, this was a task that typically fell to the children. One day, while beating sticks to make a commotion to chase away the little critters, Vailet caught the distant movement of someone, or some thing, coming towards her. Suddenly, she looked down to see a large rock python coiled inches from her feet with its mouth stretched wide preparing to strike. Without warning, the snake leaped high into the air in its attempt to reach the little girl.

"I knew I had to run away as fast as I could," she says. My heart was racing. How could a young child possibly hope to outrun such a deadly viper? It would not have been possible except for God's intervention, she tells me. It does appear that on this day, he gave one young child supernatural ability to race to safety. "He will not let your foot slip—he who watches over you will not slumber" (see Psalm 121:3).

It was providential that Vailet's sisters eventually married Christian men, because it was through their union that the entire family was introduced to Christianity. One by one, each member of the family accepted Christ and was baptized. Still, Vailet had much to learn about the loving God who sent his only Son to rescue her from the throes of Satan. Instruction came as she began to have the same recurring dream over and over again. "Take the Bible and read," a voice would tell her. She instinctively knew the voice came from God, or at least one of his angels sent to instruct her.

The promises she found in the Bible were put to the test many times in the ensuing years. One day, as Vailet was driving the family cows home from the watering hole, a lion suddenly appeared in front her. Even though the beast could have had his fill of both bovine and human, he singled out one cow and dragged it into the bush. On another day, Vailet and a group of classmates were walking home from school when they came to a river swollen by many days of torrential rains. They had crossed the river countless times before, but never when the waters were flowing so swiftly. Vailet thought she was strong enough to make it to the other side. She wasn't. "I drowned," she tells me matter-of-factly.

"All at once, a stranger pulled me from the river, and I revived," she adds. Who was that stranger? Only God knows, but there is little doubt that he had a hand in her rescue, just as he did on one other occasion when she was enjoying a pleasant swim in the river. Without any warning, a strong current swept her into a water-filled cave. Each time she tried to raise her head to catch a breath of air, she hit the roof of the cave. Miraculously she found her way to safety, but not before her stomach became extremely distended with all the water she had swallowed. "I should have died each of these times," she says, "but by God's grace I lived to tell you of his goodness."

There is one sensitive issue that I am curious about, and because I am Vailet's friend, I think I can ask her without offending, or embarrassing her. "Did your mother circumcise you when you were young?" I ask. "Yes, and it was very, very painful," she says. She explains that the usual age for girls to undergo the passage into adulthood is around 9 or 10 years of age.[2] In those days, there was no medicine available to dull the pain, so the mothers liberally applied a paste of herbs and honey. Although it burned terribly, the mixture did have therapeutic healing properties. Vailet vowed that if she ever had daughters, she would never subject them to the pain she was forced to endure.

Sadly, many young girls still die due to excessive bleeding following these procedures. Those that don't die are disfigured for life, and will likely spend the rest of their days suffering for a decision that was probably not their own.[3] Despite the risks, mothers continue to think that if their girls aren't circumcised, no man will want to marry them. Absent that, they will have little choice but to turn to prostitution to make a living. No marriage, no grandchildren. No grandchildren, no one to care for the parents in their latter years. It's as simple as that.

I ask Vailet if anyone ever took a stand against female genital mutilation (FGM), or other superstitious practices like these when she was young. She nods her head and relates how her primary school missionary teachers changed the minds of at least some parents concerning the removal of their children's bottom front teeth. They understood that the reasons for doing so were varied. For instance, some parents chose to remove their child's teeth early because they knew it would make giving fluids easier when he or she inevitably contracted tetanus. For others, it was merely a form of decoration, or a symbol to identify the child with a particular tribe. Among those who adhered to such a practice were the Wagogo, Masai, Wakagulu, Irangi, and the Barabaig tribes.

While this custom was widely accepted among the people at that time, the teachers noticed how difficult it was for the students to speak correctly without their full complement of teeth. They cleverly applied logic by telling the parents who insisted on their children learning to speak English, "Your children will not be able to pronounce the words correctly without all their teeth." This was reason enough for some children to escape an inevitable fate.

Simple things like this often spell the difference between a good and a bad outcome. Take the effectiveness of religious tracts, for instance. When Vailet was pregnant with Lilian, a woman she remembers only as Mrs. Jackson gave her two small pamphlets. One entitled, "The Heart of Paku," offered a simple, but powerful visual of what Vailet called, "the bad things of the devil." Two hearts were drawn side by side. Inside one were many dangerous animals. The other simply contained a picture of Jesus. Vailet immediately understood that if Jesus was in her heart, no bad things could exist there.

In spite of knowing this, Vailet unwittingly opened the door to the enemy years later when she began to hear voices instructing her to make beer called *wujimbi* in Cigogo.[4] "According to our culture at that time," she explains, "you could not be considered a perfect wife if you didn't make beer." After a time, other voices demanded that she stop making the intoxicating brew. "We will destroy you. We will destroy your house; we will destroy everything. Don't cook beer!" That was enough to frighten her, and eventually lead her to her pastor's house for prayer. For the first time in many years, Vailet felt free. It was as if a heavy blanket had been lifted from her shoulders. 'I am healed!' she cried. "I am healed!"

Vailet's husband continued to come home reeking of beer. "I didn't like that smell," she says, "so I didn't want him to be intimate with me." His reaction was to turn to another woman, as Lilian recounted earlier in some detail. His betrayal caused Vailet to descend into deep darkness. She freely admits it was only by God's grace that she was delivered of all the demons that controlled her every movement and thought. When Jesus came into her heart this time, all the bad animals (demons) made a hasty retreat.

One night, many years later, Vailet dreamed she heard a voice instructing her to go to the church and clean it thoroughly. Important visitors were coming. "The church was very, very dirty," she remembers. Before long, a big car arrived with the Bishop and one other man. "Why is God's house dirty?" the Bishop asked. She answered confidently and rather boldly, "If I was a church elder, it would have been cleaned before now." With that, the men left. The very next month, Vailet was elected to serve as an elder, a position she held for the next 16 years before stepping aside to chair the Sunday school department. Today, she continues to care for the children and serve in the choir as well as on the evangelism outreach team. It is not unusual for people to call on her all hours of the day or night for healing prayer. It appears that she is still very much a spiritual "medicine woman."

In 1991, Vailet was summoned to the village of Chinyika to sit by her dying mother's bedside. "Today I have a journey," she told her daughter. "Please cook *ugali* and *mlenda* (a dish made with okra and chopped pumpkin leaves) for me to eat on my journey." Thinking her mother was merely dreaming, Vailet did not hurry to prepare the food. "Vailet. I have told you to cook soon," her mother said when her daughter didn't immediately comply. "I see your Dad, your aunt, my uncle and many, many people standing on the other side of a lake," she said. "They are singing and beating drums as they wait for me. They are very happy." Upon hearing this, Vailet took her more seriously, and began to prepare the food. As she was pounding nuts to cook with the mlenda, she heard her mother snoring loudly. "Mom! Mom!" she called repeatedly. "Wake up!" Finally, her mother said weakly, "Huh?" Her voice seemed to come from far away. Vailet leaned close to her mother's ear to call her once more, but she was already gone.

As Lilian translates this story, I ask if her grandmother, or any of the other people around the lake, were Christian. "My grandmother, grandfather and my mother's sister-in-law were believers even though they still followed many of the traditional religious practices," she says. "The others never had an opportunity to hear the gospel message. Surely, God is merciful even in such circumstances. His grace is a deep mystery far beyond my comprehension."

Can you fathom the mysteries of God?
Can you probe the limits of the Almighty?
They are higher than the heavens above—what can you do?
They are deeper than the depths below—what can you know?
Their measure is longer than the earth and wider than the sea.

Job 11:7-9

NOTES

1. Joseph Healey and Donald Sybertz, Towards An African Narrative Theology (New York: Orbis Books, 1996), 22.

2. The practice of female genital mutilation (FGM) or female genital cutting or circumcision predates the birth of Islam. As such it has taken on a dimension of the religion. However, it is performed across cultures and religions and is considered not only a religious practice, but also a cultural one. http://www.mtholyoke.edu/~mcbri20s/classweb/.../page1.htm (accessed June 18, 2016).

3. Female Genital Mutilation (FGM) is recognized internationally as a violation of the human rights of girls and women according to the World Health Organization (WHO). It includes procedures that intentionally alter or cause injury to the female genital organs for non-medical reasons. Mostly carried out on young girls between infancy and age 15, FGM procedures can cause severe bleeding and problems urinating. Cysts, infections and complications in childbirth FGM may also result. The WHO reports that more than 200 million girls and women alive today have been cut in 30 countries in Africa, the Middle East and Asia alone. World Health Organization, February 2016. www.who.int/mediacentre/factsheets/fs241/en/ (accessed February 20, 2016).

4. Making beer requires filling clay pots with water and millet. These are then placed on a pit of firewood where they are left to bubble and begin the fermentation process. The entire procedure varies according to geographic location, but it usually involves malting, drying, milling, souring, boiling, mashing and fermenting in one form or another.

EPILOGUE

Delight yourself in the Lord;
And He will give you the desires of your heart.
Commit your way to the Lord, Trust also in Him,
and He will do it.

Psalm 37:4-5

Famed writer and theologian, Frederick Buechner, has said that our best dreams and truest prayers come from the Kingdom of God. "We glimpse it at those moments when we find ourselves being better than we are and wiser than we know. We catch sight of it when at some moment of crisis a strength seems to come to us that is greater than our own strength. The Kingdom of God is where we belong. It is home, and whether we realize it or not, I think we are all of us homesick for it."[1]

How right he is. God has responded to my deepest longings by fashioning a life far better than any I might have envisioned for myself. I realize the path I have chosen is not for everyone. Some are even perplexed by it. I have lived long enough to know, however, that what often makes little sense to the human mind makes perfect sense to God. He sends his wind to blow wherever he pleases to do something in us and through us that we cannot do for ourselves. "You hear its sound, but you cannot tell where it comes from or where it is going," (John 3:8b). It is unexpected. It is surprising. It is beautiful and, oh, so satisfying.

Someone, I can't recall who, once said that the fabric of our lives is intricately woven by every act of obedience, every step of faith. Chance encounters turn out to be divine appointments. God uses even the tangled threads and knots of our failures and weaknesses to produce a reflection of his glory that is unique to each one of us. He lets nothing go to waste, but works everything for the good of those "who have been called according to

109

his purpose," (Romans 8:28). What I naively assumed would be a one-time mission trip to Africa in 2007, has since turned into an enduring passion as God continues to use this land and its people to enlarge my understanding of what it means to respond to the Great Commission...of what it means to belong to a universal body of believers who serve him by showing love and compassion for one another. Africa has also opened my eyes to the spiritual world where things are not always as they seem.

For example, near the end of our initial visit to Tanzania in 2007, Lilian asked me to accompany her to her new office at Msalato Theological College where she was about to assume duties as the registrar for the upcoming semester. To date, she had not been able to make herself unlock the door to set up her offices. Each time she reached out to put her hand on the doorknob, a deep dread spread over her, preventing her from entering. She didn't know why, but she was certain that evil spirits inhabited the room. As it turned out, I had packed a bottle of anointing oil intending to leave it with our hosts for those times when they were called to pray for the sick. However, I knew this was the perfect use for this blessed element, so I grabbed the small vial, and together we set out across the campus.

Before we even opened the door, I anointed the doorframe and knob, and prayed to break any curses, hexes or spells sent against Lilian, the students, or the school. I declared them null and void. Once inside, Lilian joined me in repeating this prayer throughout the room. We held each other's hands as we broke all assignments of spirits sent against her. We quickly followed through by asking the Holy Spirit to take up residence within the office. As we continued to pray, a holy hush filled the room causing us to weep. It was evident that a deep cleansing was taking place, almost as if we had opened the windows to a fresh ocean breeze. We then offered a prayer of dedication for the office space and all those who would pass through the door during the school year ahead. The prayers came from us with such force, that when they were over, we were completely spent. With exhaustion, however, came sweet peace, and the assurance that all was well.

A few weeks after returning to the States, I received an email from Lilian. She said from the moment we prayed the cleansing prayer, she never again felt any hesitation, or fear when entering her office. Whatever evil had invaded the territory was no longer present. The office was now a blessed and sacred space, indeed. It would be several years before we would have the opportunity to return to Tanzania again, but that experience taught me much about standing firm in the face of any scare tactics the enemy might try to use against us. Little did I realize that I had much more to learn about the enemy's wiles.

In 2012, my husband and I planned a return trip to Tanzania to coincide with Given's consecration as the new Bishop of Kondoa. For the first few days, we roomed at a Catholic hostel until more suitable arrangements could be made. Early one morning, before we moved to a new location, I was awakened by a disturbing dream. Strangely enough, it continued to play out even as I lay fully awake watching the terrible scene unfold before my eyes. The following is an excerpt from my journal giving the account of that event.

In the darkest hour just before dawn—a time when only stealthy creatures of the night move about—a hyena hoping to snag a goat or chicken, a nearby rooster gearing up for his piercing morning wake-up call—the melodic sounds of the Muslim call to prayer penetrated my sleep. I was not quite awake, but somewhere in between where dreams merge with wakefulness. It was in this transition place that I found myself praying with an urgency I did not understand.

As I lay still, a scene began to come into focus in front of me. A gray haze enveloped people who were moving slowly, methodically about as if in a drugged stupor. In the foreground, a large hooded black mamba was raised, swaying hypnotically in time to the Islamic chant. It was haunting and eerily soothing, yet at the same time dark and malevolent. I was aware that this was no dream, but a vision of sorts that I was being made aware of through senses that were not my own. As the scene slowly faded away, I was left with the certainty that I had witnessed something very real just beyond the pale of mortal awareness.

A day or so later, I received a message from our intercessory prayer coordinator describing a strange turn of events at home. While at the gym one day, a snake slithered into the back of a room filled with exercising women causing them to scatter in fear. My friend moved closer to see the intruder stretched out next to the wall. As she looked down at it, my face and that of my husband appeared before her. She understood this to mean that we must be in some kind of danger, and that she was being called to plead for our protection. As she did so under her breath, a woman calmly approached the snake, and reaching for its tail with one hand while grasping it behind the head with the other, she took it outside and let it slither off into the bushes. Several days later, my friend inquired about the woman, but no one seemed to know her. They had never seen her at that facility before, and they never saw her again. An angel, perhaps?

After telling Lilian about my dream and the strange snake in the gym, she consulted her mother, who, as a result of her own experiences with evil forces, was especially perceptive in matters of spiritual warfare. Her advice was to remain vigilant, and at the same time, ask God to reveal any scheme of the enemy working against us. The following morning, I felt compelled to open our workshop with a special prayer of protection against hexes, curses, or spells that may have been cast against us by someone involved in the dark arts. Given stood beside me interpreting every word and line with equal intensity and authority. No one but us understood why we were praying so forcefully, but it was clear the class participants understood that the enemy was involved in some way. Their powerful prayers rose with ours, and for a time, we did battle together. Still, Lilian and I continued to watch and wait.

Several days after the second workshop ended, we had an opportunity to visit a distant congregation. As we drove home from the service later that evening, we passed a group of mud huts situated on either side of the road. Just outside a rundown bar with several men loitering about, Lilian spotted something alongside the road. By the time she alerted us, we were well past it. "It was a dead snake," she announced. I asked if she could identify the kind of snake. "It was a black mamba," she said without hesitation even though she admitted later that she had no idea what a mamba looked like. "It was beaten too many times." I knew this was her way of saying the men in the village had likely beaten it to death with large sticks. The significance of its position seemed especially significant. It lay twisted and torn with belly exposed as if in defeat.

It is interesting that both of us identified the snakes we saw as black mambas even though they were gray in color. When I researched black mambas after returning home, I was astounded that our assessment was correct. The black mamba is actually gray, but is so named because the inside of its mouth is black

Could this be the sign we had requested? We believed it was. God showed us that the snake in my vision and the snake in the gym were meant to alert us to "be strong in the Lord and in the strength of His might" and to put on the full armor of God so that we would be able to stand against the devil's schemes (Ephesians 6:10-11). The snake on the side of the road was a visible sign to us that God had gone before us to protect us.

We may never understand what Satan had planned, but we are confident that our prayers, and those of our intercessors at home, thwarted whatever evil had been set in motion against us. The dead serpent offered powerful proof that Satan had been turned back even as he will one day be defeated for all time. Until that time, we will continue to be on guard and do what we can to break the chains that keep so many enslaved.

Several years ago, we were introduced to a curriculum produced by Empower International Ministries, an organization established to combat the root causes of abuse, abandonment and injustice in countries where people are often marginalized by the powerful few.[2] Carrie Miles, Empower's founder, who also serves as president and executive director, offered to give us training on facilitating workshops for pastors, lay pastors, and spouses using her workbook, "New Man, New Woman, New Life."[3] We have been privileged to use this curriculum for a number of years now, and continue to hear testimonies about the amazing transformation occurring in the lives of those who attend these sessions.

The legacy of such biblically based ministries is most clearly seen in family interactions. Men who attend the workshops no longer feel that helping their wives with chores, or childcare diminishes their manhood. It is truly amazing to witness the changes taking place as men and women alike finally understand that Jesus came to set the captives free, not just from sin, but also from any kind of bondage that would keep them from living the joyful, peace-filled life he promised to those who follow him.

Martin Luther understood this. In his 1520 treatise *On Christian Liberty*, Luther said, "A Christian man is the most free lord of all, and subject to none; a Christian man is the most dutiful servant of all, and subject to everyone." Rather than being forced to submit to one another, the Christian man freely chooses to serve others. This is "the truth [that] will set you free" (John 8:32). This is, after all, a glorious theme of the gospel message, is it not? When we live in this freedom, we discover that "our redemption, our joy, our peace, and our love for each other [will] permeate our lives to such an extent that we become the light of the world, a city on a hill that cannot be hidden."[4]

During a recent trip to a rural African village, we caught up with a familiar looking priest, an Anglican canon. I couldn't quite remember where, or when I had seen him before, but I knew that our paths had crossed before. It wasn't until we sat together at lunch some hours later that I was finally able to place where I had seen this godly man. At one point during the conversation around the table I heard him say the words, *Mume Mpya, Mke Mpya, Maisha Mapya* (New Man, New Woman, New Life). Lilian leaned over to complete the translation. "We must always live as new men and women just as we were taught." The canon grasped his wife's hand, and held it high above his head with a broad smile on his face. Now I knew where I had first met this dear man of God. He was in our very first class of the "New Man, New Woman, New Life" seminar in 2012. I realized that his wife was the same woman who had unknowingly launched a remarkable new ministry for women in the diocese.

It was during a breakout session that year that I had taken special notice of her. She was not participating, but was sitting quietly with eyes averted and head bowed. I took Lilian aside to ask if the pastor's wife was literate. One thing led to another, and before long we discovered there were several others who could neither read nor write. As a direct result, the Women's Empowerment Center was established a year later on the diocesan compound—a place where young wives and mothers, and even an occasional male, are invited to come for six months of literacy, Bible and life-skill training classes.

Wherever we go in our ministry throughout Tanzania, we witness Christians graciously serving one another—selflessly, joyfully, no strings attached. One particular example stands out. It was shortly after completing an intensive interactive workshop that I began to feel very ill. Dan and I were staying at a newly built house that was yet to be occupied by its owner, a government official who was also an enthusiastic follower of Jesus Christ. The cinder block house was located just down the hill from the Bishop's residence. As was our custom, we usually walked up the hill to share each meal with the Gaula family in their home. At first, I tried to hide the fact that I was not feeling well, but it quickly became apparent that something was terribly wrong. Too weak to even raise my arms, I was forced to go to bed.

Late that evening, the whole family, including Given, Lilian, her sister, Pendo, their children, as well as Vailet and Melina, came to my room to examine me for themselves. It didn't take long before they agreed on a diagnosis. "You have malaria," they announced. I supposed they had seen it enough to know the difference between that and the flu. In fact, Ilumbo, their daughter, was recovering from a bout of it herself.

Shortly before midnight, I was wrapped in a blanket and taken to the local dispensary. Sure enough, the blood work came back positive. For several days, I could eat nothing but a thin porridge flavored with the lemony extract from the seeds of the ancient, majestic Baobob tree.[5] Nothing else would stay down.

A couple of nights later, as everyone gathered at the Gaula house for supper, I felt a strong urge to get dressed and walk up the hill to join them. I was still weak and very shaky, so rather than take the longer, but more easily traversed road, I chose a more direct route through tall weeds praying that no snakes were lying in wait to strike me.

I have a vivid memory of walking into an empty living room. "Where is everyone?" I wondered. I decided to go down the long hallway to find the source of the muffled voices I heard. I spotted activity in the room at the end of the hall. As is the case in most kitchens, there was no stove, no cupboards, nothing to identify it as a kitchen except several cooking pots placed directly over a mound of red, hot coals.

I quietly approached the room to see Vailet and Melina sitting on low, hand-carved stools peeling vegetables and stirring bubbling pots of food. I will never forget the moment they both looked up to see me standing in the doorway. Instead of coming to greet me, they immediately stood to their feet with arms stretched high above their heads. I needed no translator to know they were praising God for raising me from my sick bed. Lilian walked in to explain that both mothers had pledged not to eat another bite of food until I was able to do the same. Tears of joy accompanied the tight embraces that followed. Their sacrifice on my behalf was truly humbling.

Africa has changed me in ways I don't yet fully understand. It has enlarged my heart and my capacity to love. I appreciate how Richard Dowden, director of the Royal African Society, so aptly describes the counter culture experience. "Westerners arriving in Africa for the first time often find themselves suddenly cracked open. They lose inhibitions, feel more alive, more themselves, and they begin to understand why, until then, they have only half lived."[6] I have found that to be the case. Tanzania is where I feel most at home, where I am my best me. I recently heard a returning short-term missionary say he didn't know if he was returning home, or leaving home. Indeed. It is like having a foot in two worlds and longing for one while being physically present in the other.

Although cultural differences are many and must not be discounted, Christ's Spirit proves to be the common denominator. It is he who "enables us to be present to culture and to God who is present in it."[7] He calls us to do things we think are impossible, or at least those things we shy away from. It is only in obeying the call that we find he is the one who does the impossible. We are simply the conduits for his work. Allow me to illustrate.

Two years ago, my husband and I arrived at the Arusha/Kilimanjaro airport late in the evening. After many hours of flying followed by a long and jarring car ride to Kondoa, we were finally able to put our feet up and sleep in a real bed. Given wasted no time in putting us to work the next day, however. He asked my husband to accompany him to a number of congregations where, as Bishop, he would preside over baptisms and confirmations. Lilian and I remained behind to attend Sunday morning worship services at Church of the Good Shepherd located on the diocesan compound. We agreed to meet in Dodoma the following day to enjoy a few days of rest before traveling back to Kondoa to begin our two weeks of ministry.

Following Sunday worship services, Lilian and I were invited to share a meal with a number of the other church leaders. Before making our way across the compound to the large room where steaming pots of delicacies awaited, Lilian informed me that several expectant mothers were waiting for special prayer in the pastor's office. They had traveled long distances to be near the only medical facility anywhere around. They knew all too well that many women and babies don't survive the birthing process without adequate medical care, and they wanted to give their babies, and themselves, a fighting chance.

I wish I could say I was eager to comply, but I was exhausted after so many hours of travel from the States. All I wanted to do was take a nap. Besides, I knew these ladies wouldn't understand a word I said. When I suggested to Lilian that she be the one to offer prayer, she was clearly having none of it. Then when I reminded her needlessly that I didn't speak their language, she said, with complete confidence, I might add, that, "They don't need to understand what you say. God will translate." Properly chastened, I followed her into the small room. I'll never forget the moment I saw the four very pregnant women standing in a line before me respectful, but shy. One woman was so large that I thought she might be carrying triplets. "How does she manage to stand upright?" I wondered. I remembered my own challenge of carrying twins many years before, so I knew how uncomfortable she must be.

Obedient, but definitely feeling inadequate for the task, I opened my mouth. An amazing thing happened! The presence of the Holy Spirit completely filled the room with a kind of holy awe. Surely this was sacred ground. Everyone began to weep. I could hardly pray between sobs, and was certain the floor would soon be covered with tears that were coursing down our cheeks unimpeded. Although these ladies didn't understand a word I said, they did know the language of the Spirit. It didn't matter that we couldn't communicate with words. It didn't matter that we came from different cultures and traditions. All that mattered was that the Holy Spirit provided "the ground of the meeting between the Gospel and culture."[8] I am convinced that on this day I was privileged to sample a little of what Christ's followers must have experienced on the Day of Pentecost so long ago.

I often wondered what happened to these women, but it wasn't until we visited the following year that I had an opportunity to inquire about them. In a tone that spoke volumes, Lilian reported that all were safe and well. Why would I doubt it? After all, "The one who calls you is faithful, and he will do it" (1 Thessalonians 5:24). God honored even my tiny mustard seed of faith to perform a life-honoring miracle for each of his precious daughters that day.

A few days later, I had the privilege of praying for a young Masai mother with a baby strapped on her back. She had accompanied her other son into the forest earlier in the day for the circumcision rite of passage known as *emuratare*.[9] There the young boys would be required to pass a series of challenges. But when the mother learned of our arrival, she returned to the village to ask us to pray for her seriously ill child.

As the Bishop and I prepared to pray, I noticed two deeply indented circles on her cheeks. I asked Lilian about the depressions and was told that although many Masai embrace Christianity, they still retain certain cultural practices. In this case, the mother had burned holes in the baby's cheeks to allow the high fever to dissipate. I cringed thinking what this child must have gone through in addition to being so sick. The wounds were healed, so obviously the little one had been sick for quite some time. In truth, I doubted the child would make it through the night in the forest. Nevertheless, I prayed for her asking God to show his mercy and favor. We left shortly after the mother returned with her child to the forest. The next year, I remembered to ask Lilian if the baby survived. It was a tremendous relief to hear that healing had, indeed, taken place, and that the child was not only alive, but was thriving.

Later, I was witness to another wondrous mystery of God's love as I learned firsthand that he actually grieves for the lost. My husband and I had just concluded two long days of interactive workshops for clergy and their spouses. We planned to take an extra day to accompany Given and Lilian to Bugutole, a remote village where the diocese hoped to establish a new church. Given was especially excited because many new tribes were moving into this area from the west making it a prime region for evangelistic outreach.

For some unknown reason, the area was overrun with aggressive, venomous snakes. It was such a problem that one American who visited the area later mailed back a medical kit to treat snakebite victims. A special treatment center was set up in Farkwa about 90 minutes southwest of Kondoa. This one act of compassion saved many lives and opened the door to the gospel message.

I listened to this account and found myself strangely eager to visit the area. It seems curiosity overcame my life-long fear of snakes. Still, I knew it wasn't without risk, so I sent a special prayer request to our intercessory prayer team at home. In a matter of minutes, the prayer coordinator responded with a question. Could this unusual concentration of so many poisonous snakes be an indication of demonic influence, or control? If so, that might explain why it had been so inaccessible to Christianity. Regardless, I knew we would certainly have to fit ourselves with the full armor of God before entering what might very well be enemy territory.

As it turned out, Given and Lilian had to travel without us so that we could have time to prepare for the upcoming seminar sponsored by the Anglican Sharing of Ministries Abroad (SOMA USA) mission agency.[10] The night before they were scheduled to leave for Bugutole, Given and Lilian received devastating news. A senseless massacre had just taken place with people being driven into the forest under a hail of poison-tipped spears and arrows. They learned that the conflict erupted after local officials illegally evicted the Sandawi people from land their tribes had occupied for generations in order to sell it to a group of Sukuma migrating from the west. When they arrived on the scene, Given and Lilian were met by the overwhelming stench of death coming from the forest. The authorities might not have bothered to investigate had it not been for Given's insistence that they immediately come to arrest the perpetrators, including the corrupt officials who pocketed the money from property that wasn't theirs to sell.

After spending a long, exhausting day with the police and surviving family members, Given and Lilian began their return trip back to Kondoa. On the way, the old Land Rover slid off the dirt road coming to a rest in a deep ditch. It was hours before they were able to push the vehicle back onto the road. They arrived shortly before dawn, tired and dirty. After catching a few hours of sleep, they joined the seminar already in progress. Their eyes were filled with despair and their shoulders weighted with defeat. What had promised to be the beginning of a glorious new work for God in Bugutole, was wiped out in a matter of hours. People were already fleeing the area. It was only a matter of time before all the huts were abandoned, and the vegetation left to swallow the fields.

It was obvious we couldn't proceed as if nothing had happened. Our team along with the seminar participants, gathered around the Bishop and his wife to pray. As we laid hands on them, a great crescendo of supplication thundered through the room. I found a place behind Given, and as I reached out to touch him, great gulping sobs erupted from someplace deep inside me. I was overwhelmed with what had taken place and for what my friends had witnessed. It wasn't until later that the SOMA director, our team leader for the mission, helped me understand that what I was feeling was not the Gaulas' anguish, but rather the Father's grief that so many souls had been violently thrust into eternity before ever hearing his name. For the first time, I truly understood the words, "We do not know what we ought to pray for, but the Spirit himself intercedes for us through wordless groans... the Spirit intercedes for God's people in accordance with the will of God" (Romans 8:26b; 27b).

After praying for Given, I walked to where Lilian sat alone with her head bowed. It was here that I experienced the profound mystery of incarnation theology as Christ became flesh through one white woman (me) in order to wrap his loving arms around one African daughter (Lilian). No words were spoken, nor were they necessary.

Skeptics might try to explain away the murderous rampage in Bugutole as just another example of the tribal warfare that's been going on for centuries. They might even attribute the safe labor and delivery of the four pregnant women to the wonders of medical care albeit in a third world country. While both are true to a degree, there is much more to the story. As Christians, we know that the underlying cause for tribal unrest and the high mortality rate in childbirth are evidence of a spiritual battle that rages as our ancient adversary intensifies efforts to prevent Christ's light from breaking the spiritual chains of these people. We also know that victory ultimately belongs to God. Just this year, we learned that tribes are returning to Bugutole, something we once thought impossible. Today, in place of that terrible bloodshed and sorrow, there is a thriving congregation of 150 believers. Their presence has brought light into the darkness and with it "the oil of joy instead of mourning, and a garment of praise instead of a spirit of despair" (Isaiah 61:3a).

Still, the battle rages on. The enemy continues to pillage and plunder and capture as many souls as possible. (See John 10:10a). He uses vile deceptions and ignorance to set one man against another. In sub-Sahara Africa, for instance, people suffering from albinism are regularly hunted down like animals. Many believe their body parts have magical powers when used in potions and certain ritualistic rites. Even their graves are desecrated, and their bones used for good luck, or black magic.

A UN report dated March 22, 2016, calls attention to a recent surge in this heinous practice, and advises that education is the key to ending such superstitious practices.[11] For now, the government has established settlement enclaves to protect the hunted from the hunter. Even though security guards patrol the grounds, people are still being abducted, or hacked to death inside the gates. Even though the writer of the article identifies the root cause as superstition, we know that Satan is behind it all. He is the author of all lies and wrong thinking, every kind of struggle for power or authority, every effort to subjugate women, children, and even men, by others in positions of influence and power.

Kondoa faces many other challenges, including those imposed by the geography. It is located between the fertile territories of the northwest and the eastern coastline. For its more than 600,000 people located throughout extremely remote areas, Kondoa alternately endures floods and drought, feast and famine. When crops shrivel and die for lack of rain, so too, do the livestock who have no water to drink or grass to eat. With the floods come rushing waters that wash away the topsoil and decimate the fields.

Today, Kondoa houses one of the most influential centers for Islam in all of Central and East Africa. Although Muslims in outlying villages co-exist peacefully with Christians for now, the threat from radical Muslims on Zanzibar against opposing tribes in Kondoa is very real. At the same time, the infiltration of foreign Jihadists, and the

> Approximately 35 percent of the population in Tanzania is Muslim, but that figure rises to well over 90 percent in Kondoa. The largest concentration of Muslims are found on the island of Zanzibar where they make up approximately 95 percent of the population. Islam first spread from Arabia to Tanzania in the thirteenth century as dynastic settlements were established along the coast and further inland along pre-colonial trade routes.

return of Tanzanian radicals trained outside the country also pose a danger to moderate Muslims and Christians alike. It is the goal of church leaders like Bishop Gaula, and other godly men and women, to build bridges of understanding and compassion.

Adherents to African Traditional Religions that embrace animism, belief in ancestral spirits, and black magic, represent a smaller percentage of the population with only 15 to 20,000 people claiming to be Christian. Superstition abounds everywhere.[12] Extreme poverty, lack of access to natural resources and adequate schools make it difficult for the government to find teachers and medical personnel to fill positions. This presents a paradoxical dilemma. Kondoa needs teachers, but the teachers are reluctant to subject their own children to the existing inferior education system there. This will be a problem for the foreseeable future.

It is not just the substandard education system that keeps teachers and administrators away, though. According to Bishop Given, the number one reason people refuse to come to Kondoa is the recognition of a pervasive presence of evil. It is palpable; it is real, and for many, it is terrifying. However, God is raising up a new generation of indigenous missionaries unafraid to raise Christ's standard high as they push back the darkness to evangelize their own people. At a time when so many young people choose to flee their villages for better opportunities in the cities, or even in other countries, some feel called to stay where they are to improve the spiritual and physical lives of their neighbors. For this reason, it is especially gratifying to watch as the Gaula children prepare to step into their own God-given destinies. Ihewa, the Gaulas' eldest child, is studying to be a cardiologist. It will be a blessed day when she finally completes her studies to begin treating those who desperately need her care. As for the younger Ilumbo and Amani, they are just now exploring what God has in store for them. We will continue to watch with hopeful anticipation as they answer God's call to enrich and enlarge his vineyard in Tanzania.

Years before, Lilian dreamed of many sick children waiting to see a doctor. Although she was moved with compassion herself, she somehow sensed the doctors and nurses were not. Providing medical care was simply a job to them. Lilian began to pray for a spirit of compassion to be poured upon all those whose hands touch the sick. Later on, she had another dream in which her daughter, Ihewa, fearlessly used her own hands to kill a black mamba. In the dream, Lilian prayed that the Lord would allow her daughter to use those same hands to heal the people in Jesus Name. It is apparent that compassion and a desire to bring wholeness to others will continue to be a part of this family's rich spiritual heritage. It will be interesting to see what paths the other children choose in the years ahead.

While it is true that Satan is powerful, we know our God is more powerful still. This was driven home to us during our most recent trip to Kondoa in 2016. Along with the Gaula family and another senior priest, we were packed into the diocese's new 10-passenger Land Cruiser, the vehicle our own church, Christ Community Church in Pinehurst, North Carolina, and others, had so enthusiastically raised funds to purchase just a few months prior to our visit. Our goal was to reach Mpendo to take part in the dedication of a newly inscribed cornerstone for the church building. The trip was, well, almost indescribable. As we drove along, the hard dirt road got narrower and bumpier. The floods of the previous rainy season had washed away the sides of the road leaving dangerously steep drop-offs to navigate between.

As we progressed deeper into the thick, tangled bush, Given regaled us with the rich, but terrible history of the road. He explained that this was the actual road used by slave traders during the height of the east Africa Arab-run slave and ivory trade orchestrated by the Sultan of Oman from his capital located on the island of Zanzibar. The port city of Bagamoyo served as Zanzibar's gateway to the interior of Africa. For the slaves, however, it represented a one-way ticket to a life of forced servitude as shackled slaves were auctioned off to Indian and European slave traders before being taken to India, Persia, and South Africa. Some were only marginally more fortunate. They were sold to owners who lived and operated on the east African coast.

Regardless of where they ended up, life as they had known it was over. The name, Bagamoyo, is made up of the word "Moyo" which means a slowing of the heart. The captives knew that once they reached this city, the beat of their own African hearts would cease. They would never again see their friends and family. Slavery was only abolished in Tanganyika in 1922, so the town of Bagamoyo still retains evidence of its sad history. In fact, many of the town's residents are direct descendants of slave traders, owners, porters, and even the slaves themselves.

Given continued to talk at length while I tried to envision the long caravan of humans wending their way through the bush, heartbroken and frightened. I wanted to take notes, but the rough roads made it impossible. At one point, Given told us to quickly roll up our windows. We were in tsetse, or as it is sometimes called, tik-tik fly territory. These large biting parasite-spreading flies are found in much of the mid-continental Africa between the Sahara and Kalahari Deserts. No sooner had we rolled up the windows than the little buggers began attacking the windows all around. It was amazing really, almost like something out of a horror film. This was definitely no-man's land except for poachers who somehow continue to trade in elephant tusks despite rather large bounties on their heads.

What made this whole experience so astounding was the backstory. This same road traveled by slaves and slave traders was also the same road a poor young evangelist by the name of Given Gaula traveled many years before. Although I have already spoken of Given's difficult life as an evangelist to the people of Tarkwa, this was a piece of the story I had not heard until now. Even though his living conditions were dire, young Given persevered. He was determined not to give up without a fight, so once a month he would mount his bicycle for the 80-mile round trip to Kondoa to buy whatever meager food supplies he could afford.

As Given continued to fill in the details of those early days, my imagination soared. I could almost picture the poor young boy riding through this same area with the flies attacking him all around. When I asked how he managed to fend them off, he explained that he wove small, leafy branches to make a kind of hood to keep the flies from his face and arms during the long round trip that would take him all day and into the night to complete.

Think of it. Centuries before chained slaves marched down this same road towards what must have seemed to them to be certain death. Fast forward to the modern era with a young, black evangelist riding his bicycle over the same trail on a mission from God. Move ahead once more to today where this very faithful man is now a bishop comfortably ensconced in the relative comfort of an air-conditioned car. If that is not the grace of God, I don't know what is. Just the visual imagery of this road as the route of destruction and despair being transforming into something good, something glorious, something eternal, is worthy of praise. The road to hellish slavery has now become the road to freedom and salvation. I mentally envision the slaves and Given uniting to quote Genesis 50:20: "You intended to harm me, but

God intended it for good to accomplish what is now being done, the saving of many lives."

Scripture tells us, "The harvest is plentiful but the workers are few (Matthew 9:37b). For now, the Anglican Diocese of Kondoa remains a missionary enterprise in the truest sense of the term. Unlike much of Tanzania, and, indeed, most of Africa during the missionary era of the eighteenth century when missionaries first brought education and health services with them, Kondoa remained largely unreached until the 20th century.

Today, instead of foreigners, it is the indigenous church that is serving as missionaries to its own people. It is because they are a poor people, largely forgotten until recently, that they are in desperate need of outside resources to help evangelize, disciple, and educate those living in the rural areas. As the Bishop says, education and the gospel message civilize and transform people to live as God intended. When asked why the missionaries did not pass this way, the Bishop says he is convinced that, in God's great providence, he ordained "this to be our time to contribute to the advancement of the Kingdom of God."

This is the context of Kondoa's mission. It is not easy to work in such a closed society, but it is a rewarding work, nonetheless. Those of us who choose to walk beside our African brothers and sisters soon find we are beneficiaries more than we are benefactors.

We know that God has great plans for the people of Kondoa. It is clear the enemy does as well, but he will not win. Our victorious Christ, through his atonement on the Cross, has already won the victory! For that reason, we must continue to do everything we can to deliver "the radical Judeo-Christian idea of a God who loves us, and who asks that we love each other in return."[13] The heart cry of the Bishop, his wife, and others working alongside them, is to teach their people that Christ has come to show them a better way to live. "See, I am doing a new thing! Now it springs up; do you not perceive it? I am making a way in the wilderness and streams in the wasteland" (Isaiah 43:19).

I would like to share a story so often repeated that its origin is unclear. However, it is worth repeating here. This version is told by a North Park

University, Chicago, faculty member. It is excerpted here.

"The zookeeper set a trap, using a narrow necked jar with the monkey's favorite fruit inside. It didn't take long at all for the curious little monkey to come upon the jar that was strangely tied to a tree. Upon seeing his favorite fruit inside the little primate stuck his hand in the jar in order to grab ahold of what he wanted. Wrapping his little monkey fist around the goods, he then went to pull his hand free and found he could not. With the treats in hand, his fist was simply too large to get past the narrow opening of the jar. Pull and pull the monkey did, but he simply couldn't get free.

"Unwilling to let go of the fruit, his little monkey's fist remained stuck in the jar that was attached to a rope that was tied to a tree. And after a bit the zoo-keeper simply untied the rope from the tree and led the little monkey to the zoo with his little monkey fist still tightly wrapped around what he simply wouldn't let go."[15]

The moral of the story is that the foolish monkey could have been free to live in his jungle paradise if he had just let go of what he was holding onto so tightly. Instead, he was forever trapped, unable to enjoy life to the fullest. I, for one, am so glad I opened my fist to put my hand in that of my Savior. If I hadn't, I never would have taken part in the deliverance of the demented Masai woman who threw herself at our feet, or comforted the young wife whose husband had chewed off half her ear in a crazed, jealous rage. I never would have heard the hilarious story of the church built of straw and grasses that was there one day and gone the next all because a hungry donkey couldn't control his appetite. I never would have met Victoria, the old woman with the one long front tooth who, when asked her age, thought long and hard before replying, "Oh, I think about 1,000 years." And I certainly wouldn't have been present to witness Bishop Given laughing until tears ran down his face as he recounted one certain story of hardship in his youth that is funny only now, many years later, as he recalls his daring youthful exploits.

Perhaps most meaningful of all is the realization that if I had not been willing to follow the Spirit's prompting that took me to Africa, I would not have had the opportunity to see God fan the flames of missions already in the heart of our own granddaughter, Bethany Grace Crandall. Although she was already a veteran of numerous stateside mission endeavors, her first international trip was with her Nana and Chief (that's us) in 2016. Undaunted by unfamiliar foods, primitive dirt roads and outdoor squat toilets, she fell in love with the land and its people just as we did when we first visited Tanzania in 2007. What a joy to know that God has some very special adventures planned for our Bethy in the not-too-distant future— plans that will surely combine her love of music and missions in a most rewarding way.

Yes. I could not have guessed my future, just as Given and Lilian could not have predicted the path their lives would take. For them, it was the road to Kondoa. For me, it has also been, at least for a time, the road to Kondoa. There is One, however, to whom nothing comes as a surprise. He is the One who holds our future, and if we let him, he will take us on a grand adventure that will surpass even our wildest dreams.

> *Before I formed you in the womb I knew you,*
> *before you were born I set you apart;*
> *I appointed you as a prophet to the nations.*
>
> *Jeremiah 1:5*

NOTES

1. Buechner, Frederick. *Secrets in the Dark*, (New York: HarperCollins Publishers, 2006), p. 149.

2. Carrie Miles, a social and organizational psychologist and founder of Empower International Ministries studied African culture for many years to uncover the root cause of abuse, abandonment, and injustice. The result of her intensive studies reveals the devastating consequences of humankind's departure from God's original design for life and how both male and female have "suffered the physical consequences of living outside of God's abundant provision." Her work is detailed in her book, Miles, Carrie, *The Redemption of Love: Rescuing Marriage and Sexuality from the Economics of a Fallen World*, Brazos Press, 2006.

3. Miles, Carrie and Iannaccone, Laurence R. 2010 African edition. (Published by Empower International Ministries 2008). www.EmpowerInternational.org.

4. Miles. *The Redemption of Love*, p. 209.

5. The ancient baobab tree is an icon of the African savannah with a lifespan of up to 5,000 years. It can reach more than 98 feet high and up to 164 feet in circumference. The baobab is fittingly called a symbol of life in a landscape where little else thrives. During the rainy season it absorbs and stores water in its leaves and vast trunk enabling it to produce a nutrient-dense fruit and a bark that can be scraped for fiber to make rope, clothing and brooms. It can also serve as a shelter and food and water for both animals and humans.

6. Dowden, Richard. *Africa: Altered States, Ordinary Miracles,* (New York: Public Affairs, Perseus Books Group, 2009), p. 1.

7. Dhavamony, Mariasusal. Christian *Theology of Inculturation,* (Rome: Gregorian Biblical BookShop, 1997), p. 106.

8. Ibid., p. 106.

9. Both men and women of the Masai society have traditionally undergone the rite of circumcision that elevates them to adulthood, although fewer women are following this custom today. A few days before the operation, a boy must herd cattle for seven consecutive days with circumcision taking place before sunrise on the eighth day. He begins by allowing himself to be subjected to a cold shower. Moving towards the site where the procedures will be performed without anesthesia, his friends and male members of the family shout encouragement as well as threats and nasty looks. After an experienced male carries out the circumcision, the boy who successfully endures the procedure without flinching receives gifts of livestock from friends and relatives as a sign of respect for his bravery. The healing process takes 3 to 4 months, but the boys must remain in black cloths for a period of 4 to 8 months. Afterwards, they receive the status of a warrior. The Maasai Association. http://Maasai-association.org. (accessed June 17, 2016).

10. Sharing of Ministries Abroad (SOMA) is an international mission agency serving the Anglican Communion and the worldwide Church through short-term, cross-cultural missions both locally and abroad. As such it ministers to the clergy and lay leaders alike. SOMA: Sharing of Ministries Abroad. www.somausa.org. (accessed February 20, 2016).

11. Ero, Ikponwosa. "'Witchcraft' beliefs trigger attacks against people with albinism, UN expert warns" UN News Centre, March 22, 2016. (accessed May 16, 2016).

12. Pray Africa, a ministry of Africa Inland Mission facilitating intercessory prayer for people groups in Africa, filed a report about superstitious cattle herders and farmers known as the Rangi (Irangi) of the Kondoa Haubi highlands who do not practice witchcraft, but zealously guard an ancient sacred forest where traditional witchcraft initiation ceremonies one took place. PrayAfrica.org, January 5, 2012. (accessed January 2016).

13. Miles and Iannaccone. http://www.empowerinternational.orgweb.

14. Duane Elmer, *Cross-Cultural Connections,* (Downers Grove, IL: InterVarsity Press, 2002), p. 18.

15. *Let it go,* University Ministries. October 15, 2013. http://www.npumin.com/blog/2013/10/15/let-it-go

APPENDIX

IN LOVING TRIBUTE

Joseph Mdahe Zakaria Mwituze
(shown here with his wife, Vailet)

Born on January 1, 1940, Chinyika Mpwapwa, Tanzania
Went home to be with the Lord on September 23, 2017,
Mpwapwa Town, Tanzania

*He will wipe away every tear from their eyes, and death shall
be no more, neither shall there be mourning, nor crying, nor pain
anymore, for the former things have passed away.*

Revelation 21:4

IN LOVING TRIBUTE

Rev. Capt. David Pearce
(shown here with his wife, Jen)

Born on July 10, 1931, United Kingdom
Went home to be with the Lord on September 23, 2017,
New Zealand

Well done, good and faithful servant! You have been faithful with a few things; I will put you in charge of many things. Come and share your master's happiness!

Matthew 25:23

Bishop Given Gaula teaches a group of clergy, lay pastors (catechists) and their spouses in 2014. Photo by Kyle Spradley. Used by permission of Sharing of Ministries Abroad (SOMA USA).

Bishop Given Gaula in the liturgical vestments of his high office.

The original Gaula family home is still in use today.

Given stands inside the Gaula family home to show where his
father suspended him over a cooking fire.

Melina, Given's mother.

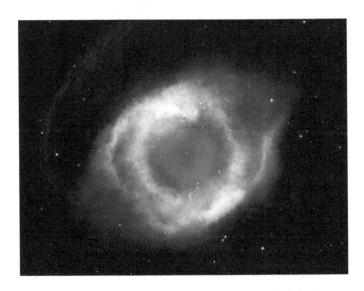

"Eye of God." Photo Credit: NASA. Used by permission.

An old photograph of Melina's fellow congregants under the tree where they held services for many years.

The congregation gathers by the same tree in 2007 with their newly erected church building in the background. Church of the Word in Gainesville, VA, raised funds for the rafters and metal roofing.

Given and Lilian, newly engaged.

Vailet, Lilian's mother.

Gaula children. Ilumbo (left), Ihewa, and Amani, 2016.

Left to right: Vailet (Lilian's mother),
Lilian, Melina (Given's mother).

Lilian Gaula is shown (right) with village women. Lilian is sometimes referred to as Mama Askofu, or Mama Bishop, or informally as Mama Ihewa, the name of her firstborn child.

Young boys emerge from the forest after completing their circumcision rite of passage.

Masai women and children greet our vehicle.

The author begins a block of instruction for a class on intercessory prayer.
Photo by Kyle Spradley. Used by permission of SOMA USA.

The author consoles Lilian shortly after the tribal massacre in Bugutole.
Photo by Kyle Spradley. Used by permission of SOMA USA.

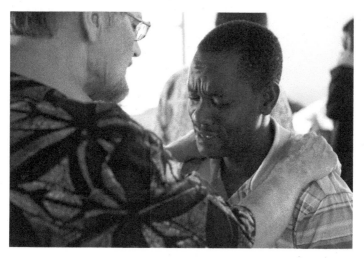

The author's husband, Dan, prays for a church leader.
Photo by Kyle Spradley. Used by permission of SOMA USA.

Dan Thomas teaches a class on integrity during a seminar for church leaders and spouses.
Photo by Kyle Spradley. Used by permission of SOMA USA.

The author and Bishop Gaula pray for a seriously ill Masai child.

Villagers gather under the thatched room of their "outdoor" church to hear
Bishop Given's sermon and to take part in confirmation rites.
Muslim leaders pay their respects by joining in the worship service.

Victoria in her rural village in 2012. When asked her age, the older
woman said she was about 1,000 years old." Painting by Ginger Martin,
cousin of the author. Used by permission.